WALKING IN
YOUR ASSIGNMENT

WALKING IN YOUR ASSIGNMENT

Finding Your Purpose and Destiny

BISHOP JOHN FRANCIS

CROSS HOUSE BOOKS
Christian Book Publishers
245 Midstocket Road
Aberdeen
AB15 5PH, UK

"The entrance of Your Word brings light."

ISBN: 978-1-910048-20-7

For Worldwide Distribution, Printed in U.S.A.

1 2 3 4 5 6 7 / 20 19 18 17 16

To order products & other Cross House Books, contact sales@crosshousebooks.co.uk.

Other correspondence: info@crosshousebooks.co.uk.

Visit www.crosshousebooks.co.uk

ACKNOWLEDGMENTS

I thank Dr. Joe Ibojie, Angela Rickabaugh Shears, and Catherine Minott for their tireless commitment in making this book happen—it would not have been possible without you.

At the synagogue in Nazareth, Jesus stood up to read from the scroll of the prophet Isaiah that was handed to Him:

"The Spirit of the Lord is on me, because he has anointed me to proclaim good news to the poor. He has sent me to proclaim freedom for the prisoners and recovery of sight for the blind, to set the oppressed free, to proclaim the year of the Lord's favor" (Luke 4:18-19 NIV).

CONTENTS

Foreword 1

Preface   The Assignment 3

Chapter 1   Your Assignment 7

Chapter 2   Why Is Love So Important? 19

Chapter 3   The Purpose of the Spirit of the Lord 29

Chapter 4   Are You Anointed? 41

Chapter 5   Sharing Good Tidings. 51

Chapter 6   Healing the Brokenhearted 61

Chapter 7   Proclaiming Liberty. 73

Chapter 8   Proclaiming the Acceptable Year of the Lord 85

Chapter 9   The Lord's Day of Vengeance. 97

Chapter 10   Set Apart for God's Service 107

Chapter 11   Rejoicing in God's Great Blessings. 117

Conclusion   What Will You Do Next? 129

FOREWORD

Bishop John Francis has been a spiritual son and dear friend to Theresa and I for many years. We love him and Pastor Penny with all our hearts. It humbles me to see how God has taken a young man who used to attend our European conferences at the Royal Albert Hall and watch our miracle working power of God in action, and now use him to build one of London's most powerful church ministries impacting so many thousands of peoples' lives every week.

Bishop John Francis is an example of how to follow a God-given assignment.

It is my great joy to recommend this book as essential for anyone who wants to fulfill their God-given assignment for their life.

God's servant,
Morris Cerullo

The Assignment

I am privileged to be the pastor of Ruach City Church where we believe that every Christian is on a journey, seeking to know the holy calling, the assignment, given to each person by Christ in line with Scripture:

*for **He delivered us and saved us and called us** with a holy calling [a calling that leads to a consecrated life—a life set apart—a life of purpose], not because of our works [or because of any personal merit—we could do nothing to earn this], but because of His own purpose and grace [His amazing, undeserved favor] which was granted to us in Christ Jesus before the world began [eternal ages ago], but now [that extraordinary purpose and grace] has been fully disclosed and realized by us through the appearing of our Savior Christ Jesus who [through His incarnation and earthly ministry] abolished death [making it null and void] and brought life and immortality to light through the gospel* (2 Timothy 1:9-10 AMP).

I use the term "assignment" to illustrate the holy calling God has placed on our lives through Christ. This literary resource will help you to discover what God has anointed you to be so that you can confidently walk in and fulfill your assignment, your calling—for His glory and advancement of His Kingdom on earth as it is in Heaven.

This "assignment" of mine has been germinating for years as I have faithfully followed God's direction, and I am so very excited to now share it with you in the form of this book. May you find your assignment and use it to praise and glorify your heavenly Father to the fullest—every day and in every way.

Chapter 1

YOUR ASSIGNMENT

Have you ever considered your everyday life as an assignment from God? Have you asked Him what is your assignment here on earth? Are you willing to discover your God-given assignment and then complete it to the best of your ability—using the talents and skills God placed within you before you were born?

According to the Oxford Dictionary, an assignment is a task or piece of work assigned to someone as part of a job or course of study; also an assignment can be a commission, mission, engagement, occupation, undertaking, exercise, business, office, and a responsibility.

Perhaps your assignment is a commission to write or paint or campaign for public office. Or maybe it is to go to the mission field and minister to people totally unlike you or your homeland. The Lord may assign you to engage someone in faith discussions, leading that person to salvation or healing. Are you to occupy a position that will change the world—or at least the world around you? What undertaking has elevated you to a higher level of spiritual understanding? Have you exercised the authority and power granted to you by the Holy Spirit to help someone out of dire straits—to help yourself become a light in a dark world?

Or perhaps your assignment is to start a business or manage an office or to take on more responsibility at your current job. You can make a difference in everyday living by knowing your God-given assignment and then pursuing it with all your heart, spirit, and mind. Let's take a look at how Jesus accepted His assignment, defined it, and then lived it.

JESUS'S ASSIGNMENT

To understand your assignment, you must understand Jesus's assignment. In the New Testament, Luke tells us that Jesus, the Son of the Living God, entered a synagogue in Nazareth on the Sabbath and was handed the scroll of Isaiah, an Old Testament prophet. Jesus unrolled the scroll and read the following:

> *"The Spirit of the Lord is upon Me (the Messiah), because He has anointed Me to **preach the good news** to the poor. He has sent Me to announce release (pardon, forgiveness) to the captives, and recovery of sight to the blind, to **set free those who are oppressed** (downtrodden, bruised, crushed by tragedy), to **proclaim the favorable year of the Lord** [the day when salvation and the favor of God abound greatly]"* (Luke 4:18-19 AMP).

Jesus's assignments were written decades before He was born of the Virgin Mary. Isaiah, who most likely lived in the 8th century BC *(Before Christ)*, wrote down all of the assignments that the coming Messiah would accomplish on earth, according to the will of God the Father.

Jesus's assignments were tasks meant to change lives. The first three assignments He read aloud that day in the synagogue:

- Preach the Good News (Gospel)
- Set free the blind and oppressed
- Proclaim the favorable year of the Lord

Jesus based His three-year ministry and fulfilled His destiny by fulfilling an Old Testament proclamation. Likewise, we can fulfill our destiny by completing our assignments as God makes them known to us. For instance, Paul wrote to the Galatians, *"let the Holy Spirit guide your lives. Then you won't be doing what your sinful nature craves"* (Galatians 5:16).

The Bible is full of wisdom for living a joy-filled, abundant life!

The Bible is full of page after page of wisdom for living a life that overflows with joy and abundance. All we have to do is seek His Kingdom and righteousness *first,* and all the good things in this life will be given to us (see Matthew 6:33). Each of us has our own particular, unique assignment. But each assignment will always be connected to God's will and the special talents and skills He created within us.

Jesus was given the ability and authority to *preach the Gospel,* the Good News, in such a way that centuries later people still feel the power of the Word, as if He is speaking directly to them even today. Jesus was also given the capacity to *heal the blind and liberate people* held captive by addiction, abuse, self-pity, poverty, and the like. Jesus *proclaimed the favorable year of the Lord* so all of God's creation would know Almighty God's infinite glory and sovereign rule over all.

Our assignments may not seem as grand as those of Jesus, but each assignment is an important part of the whole—the whole plan that God set in place before the first sunrise, before the first drop of rain, and before Adam's first breath.

> **In the beginning the Word already existed.** *The Word was with God, and the Word was God. He existed in the beginning with God. God created everything through him, and nothing was created except through him. The Word gave life to everything that was created, and his life brought light to everyone. The light shines in the darkness, and the darkness can never extinguish it* (John 1:1-5).

It is hard for us to fathom the vast, intricate, eons-long scheme of things that God put into place from before the beginning. Our finite minds can't grasp the enormity of it all. That is when faith steps in and assures us of the magnificent yet simplistic nature of God's greatness. Faith is bringing the unfathomable into the reality of our everyday lives. The tiny, tight green bud that opens into a glorious, colorful multi-petal flower. Fluffy white clouds that turn into a grey blanket wringing out moisture to nourish the earth. Seeds that produce fruit that produce seeds that produce fruit, and so on.

God's perfect plan and timing continues to amaze generation after generation—all who take the time to wonder and enjoy the miracles surrounding each of us. Perhaps each of us has a sub-assignment to point out these supernatural occurrences and spectacles, enhancing lives as well as bringing revelation of who our God truly is.

THE GREAT ASSIGNMENT

Jesus gave His disciples a specific assignment—the Great Commission—as cited in Matthew 28:18-20 (NIV):

> *Then Jesus came to them and said, "All authority in heaven and on earth has been given to me. Therefore go and make disciples of all nations, baptizing them in the name of the Father and of the Son and of the Holy Spirit, and teaching them to obey everything I have commanded you. And surely I am with you always, to the very end of the age."*

Jesus told His most trusted and closest friends and brothers in the faith to 1) make disciples, 2) baptize them, and 3) teach them. As believers in Christ, we too are His disciples and therefore Jesus tells us to make disciples by teaching people about Him and baptizing them in the name of the Father and the Son and the Holy Spirit. Doing this ensures that Jesus will be with us *"always, to the very end of the age."*

Jesus will never let you down!

That great assignment is easier for some to accomplish than others. Depending on our personality, upbringing, and training, we can be zealous for sharing the Gospel—or we can be shy. Don't worry, God will use you as you are. He knows your idiosyncrasies and will use them to bring others to Himself through you. Perhaps your quiet attitude will catch the attention of those who see your sincerity and your genuine love for the Lord in the way you treat others. Perhaps your zealousness will motivate those who are yearning for a purpose greater than themselves.

At Ruach City Church we provide varied opportunities for people to become involved in ministry, and many times they discover their assignment. Our ministries include children, youth, singles, marriage, outreach, prison ministry, mission, education, and business. For example, we have had people who have come to our church as soon as they were released from prison because their lives were changed as a result of our visits and they wanted to experience our Sunday services.

One particular person who comes to mind is a young man who attended our ministry, gave his life to the Lord, got baptized, and went on to study at our Ruach City Bible Institute and graduated. He is still pursuing education and is active in ministry. He has excelled in every area of his life that he once thought was unattainable. His whole perspective on life has changed—this is just one of many testimonies that we love to share and be part of. Our assignment is to make an impact on people's lives—one person at a time—to see lives changed, transformed, and people accomplishing all that God has intended for them.

We have also had more mature people attend the course and graduate—people in their 50s and 60s. Why did they wait so long to pursue further education? Some people felt they were not good enough to pursue higher education, whether it be secular education or some form of theology course. They might have had negative words spoken over their lives when they were younger that stuck with them for too many years, and therefore stunted their growth in that area, and some people didn't step forward until later in life because of fear. The fear of failing the course—before they even apply. Fortunately, we have found a way to help those with low self-esteem by hosting a sponsorship program. There is always someone on the waiting list to be nominated to attend the course free of charge, and the vast majority graduate.

We also have a Business Forum, which helps people maximize their business potential. Many entrepreneurs have ideas and visions but don't know exactly how to get that needed kick-start. So our Business Forum is designed to develop business strategies that support the advancement of God's Kingdom by creating sustainable and profitable Kingdom businesses globally and discipling, equipping, and empowering Christian business leaders to influence culture and create change.

Even the sky is not the limit when seeking your assignment from the Lord. His imagination and your talents and skills are dynamite that will blow the roof off any lowly expectations you may think God has in store for you. He is waiting for you to open your heart and mind and spirit so He can show you the limitless ideas and possibilities He will make available for you to take advantage of.

LIMITLESS POSSIBILITIES

Not everyone is created to be a ballerina or an accountant or a race car driver or a missionary. But everyone *is* created to share the Good News of the Gospel of Jesus Christ. And we can do that in a myriad of ways—at work and play, at night and throughout every day.

God made sharing the Gospel as easy as blinking, as breathing, as drinking a glass of water. There is no need for a PhD in theology or a degree in communications. There is no need for memorizing the Bible from cover to cover (although reading it cover to cover is definitely recommended). There is no need to study the history of the city of Pithom or be able to define a Rabshakeh. God has given you everything you need to be successful at every one of your assignments. You will have the words to say and the tools to build and the skill to craft whatever is required for your calling to be completed.

Remember how Moses balked when God told him he would lead the Israelites out of Egypt. Moses told God that he wasn't a public speaker, to which God replied:

> *"All right,"* [God] *said. "What about your brother, Aaron the Levite? I know he speaks well. And look! He is on his way to meet you now. He will be delighted to see you. Talk to him, and put the words in his mouth.* ***I will be with both of you as you speak, and I will instruct you both in what to do.*** *Aaron will be your spokesman to the people. He will be your mouthpiece, and you will stand in the place of God for him, telling him what to say. And take your shepherd's staff with you, and use it to perform the miraculous signs I have shown you"* (Exodus 4:14-17).

For every God-given assignment, you will receive whatever you need to accomplish the task. Every one.

God will give you whatever you need whenever you need it!

Joseph is a good example of God providing what was necessary for him to persevere through traumatic and dramatic times while on his journey to complete his ultimate assignment to save his family. When Joseph was tossed into the pit by his brothers and then sold into slavery, his God-given management skills made him the overseer of a well-to-do household. When he was falsely accused of rape and thrown into jail, his administrative skills moved him into a position of leadership in the prison. And when the Pharaoh's dreams required interpretation, the Lord gave Joseph insight: *"Then Pharaoh said to Joseph, 'Since God has revealed the meaning of the dreams to you, clearly no one else is as intelligent or wise as you are'"* (Genesis 41:39). Joseph then became governor of the land and managed all the food supply—his ultimate assignment was fulfilled.

And mention must be made of Mary—the mother of Jesus. Perhaps she thought of her purpose in life as she entered her teenage years. Would she be a wife, a mother, a seamstress, or other usual existences. Did she daydream about being the mother of the long-awaited Messiah? I don't know. But with God *all* things are possible and she indeed did conceive a child by the Holy Spirit and delivered a baby boy—the Prince of Peace, Immanuel. She received her assignment from the angel Gabriel and followed through to the bitter end when she witnessed her child, God's Son, crucified on the cross of salvation.

Of course Jesus fulfilled His assignment that was proclaimed by Isaiah and then confirmed by Jesus when He read from Isaiah at the Temple:

> *Then He* [Jesus] *closed the book, and gave it back to the attendant and sat down. And the eyes of all who were in the synagogue were fixed on Him. And He began to say to them,* **"Today this Scripture is fulfilled in your hearing."** *So all bore witness to Him, and marveled at the gracious words which proceeded out of His mouth...* (Luke 4:20-22 NKJV).

Jesus knew His ultimate sacrifice—the conclusion of His assignment—would be to die for the redemption of all sinners. He died a torturous, horrific death on a cross—for you and me. He accepted His assignment and although at the end He was filled with grief, He knew that He had to follow God's will for His life.

Unlike Jesus, Jonah decided he wasn't going to listen to God, he wasn't going to accept his assignment to preach to the people who lived in Nineveh. Nope. Jonah went in the opposite direction—and ran into big trouble!

The Lord gave this message to Jonah son of Amittai: "Get up and go to the great city of Nineveh. Announce my judgment against it because I have seen how wicked its people are." But Jonah got up and went in the opposite direction to get away from the Lord. He went down to the port of Joppa, where he found a ship leaving for Tarshish. He bought a ticket and went on board, hoping to escape from the Lord by sailing to Tarshish. But the Lord hurled a powerful wind over the sea, causing a violent storm that threatened to break the ship apart. Fearing for their lives, the desperate sailors shouted to their gods for help and threw the cargo overboard to lighten the ship. But all this time Jonah was sound asleep down in the hold. So the captain went down after him. "How can you sleep at a time like this?" he shouted. "Get up and pray to your god! Maybe he will pay attention to us and spare our lives" (Jonah 1:1-6).

Trying to get away from the Lord doesn't work. Never did—never will. We can't run away, we can't boat away, we can't fly away, we can't hide from God. He is with us every moment of every day. That statement of truth may be a comforting thought or a scary one depending on our everyday activities.

Finally, in the middle of a terrible storm, Jonah realized this fact and said:

"Throw me into the sea," Jonah said, "and it will become calm again. I know that this terrible storm is all my fault." Instead, the sailors rowed even harder to get the ship to the land. But the stormy sea was too violent for them, and they couldn't make it. Then they cried out to the Lord, Jonah's God. "O Lord," they pleaded, "don't make us die for this man's sin. And don't hold us responsible for his death. O Lord, you have sent this storm upon him for your own good reasons." Then the sailors picked Jonah up and threw him into the raging sea, and the storm stopped at once! The sailors were awestruck by the Lord's great power, and they offered him a sacrifice and vowed to serve him. Now the Lord had arranged for a great fish to swallow Jonah. And Jonah was inside the fish for three days and three nights (Jonah 1:12-17).

Chances are that if we go in the opposite direction God will not cause a whale of a fish to swallow us, but He can present situations that make us feel as if we are caught in the belly of a raging sea! I find Jonah's prayer most inspiring as the light turned on in his spirit and he knew how much God loved him, how much God had done for him:

> ***Then Jonah prayed*** *to the Lord his God from inside the fish. He said, "**I cried out to the Lord in my great trouble, and he answered me.** I called to you from the land of the dead, and Lord, **you heard me!** You threw me into the ocean depths, and I sank down to the heart of the sea. The mighty waters engulfed me; I was buried beneath your wild and stormy waves. Then I said, 'O Lord, you have driven me from your presence. Yet I will look once more toward your holy Temple.'*
>
> *"I sank beneath the waves, and the waters closed over me. Seaweed wrapped itself around my head. I sank down to the very roots of the mountains. I was imprisoned in the earth, whose gates lock shut forever. **But you, O Lord my God, snatched me from the jaws of death!** As my life was slipping away, I remembered the Lord. And my earnest prayer went out to you in your holy Temple. Those who worship false gods turn their backs on all God's mercies. But I will offer sacrifices to you with songs of praise, and **I will fulfill all my vows.** For my salvation comes from the Lord alone."*
>
> *Then **the Lord ordered the fish to spit Jonah out** onto the beach* (Jonah 2:1-10).

When we realize that we have not accepted our God-given assignment and the jaws of death are chomping down on us, there is only one thing, the right thing, to do—pray! Remember the Lord and pray earnestly, look into His wonderful face and repent, apologize, and tell Him exactly how you feel. He wants us to call on His name, to seek His presence. I believe that His best days were the ones before Adam and Eve disobeyed Him—the days when the three walked together in the Garden in peace and harmony with all of creation.

There are many, many stories in the Bible about assignments and how people accepted or rejected them. We can learn a great deal from each story. That's what is so wonderful, so miraculous about the Bible, God's Word. Every person who takes the time to read and absorb what is written becomes wiser and closer to

God. There are lessons to learn in every chapter, every verse—the Holy Spirit leads the way into the life-changing mysteries, revealing exciting and amazing truths.

MY ASSIGNMENT

There was a stage in my life, in my younger years, when I was a minister at my father's church. I was very active hosting revival meetings—actually they were choir rehearsals that always turned into a revival service. People would come in from the street and listen to us and many chose to give their lives to the Lord as a result. I traveled all around the world with my choir, The Inspirational Choir. Life was going sweetly, and I enjoyed the call of God on my life.

However, when my father wanted to appoint me as a pastor, life changed almost beyond my comprehension. I found out who loved me and who didn't. I heard comments such as, "Over my dead body will you be the pastor over me" and "If he becomes a pastor, I'm walking out of this church," and comments even more hurtful that I cannot repeat. The most painful for me was hearing these remarks from people whom I respected and loved. This shook me to the core and the day before my ordination to become a pastor, I wanted to run away. I wanted to pack my bags and go into hiding; but I knew deep down within myself, I couldn't run away—I wouldn't let my parents down.

So I did the next best thing and hid in my room and cried all day and night. I pleaded with God to let this situation change as I didn't want to be a pastor over people who didn't want me. Then on ordination day, we sang the song, "Thy will, Thy will be done. Oh teach me from my heart to say, Thy will be done." I was crying my eyes out and I remember saying to the Lord, "I accept Your calling of the assignment on my life."

It was then that God really spoke to me, and I realized it wasn't about how I felt or what I wanted—it was about the assignment over my life. God has blessed me with one of the fastest growing churches, with several locations throughout the United Kingdom and abroad. Had I listened to people and run from the assignment that God had on my life, I would never have experienced what God had planned for me.

Love Sweet Love

It is also hard for us to fathom the depth of the Lord's love for us, which we will look at in the next chapter.

Chapter 2

WHY IS LOVE SO IMPORTANT?

What is the basic foundation of a God-inspired life? Love. We need to have love to carry out our assignments with pure hearts.

A lot of Christians want to walk in their assignment but they don't have love in them, so they stumble along in their walk—and they won't accomplish their assignment. The truth is that you can't effectively minister to people or even have a genuine relationship with people if you don't show them love.

Too many believers want to be spiritual without having sincere love for others, which reminds me of the Corinthian church members who seemed to be proficient in spiritual gifts but didn't have love in their hearts. Apostle Paul wrote to the Corinthians explaining to them that having spiritual gifts without the presence of love means nothing: *"Prophecy and speaking in unknown languages and special knowledge will become useless. But love will last forever!"* (1 Corinthians 13:8). He even began the chapter with these words: *"If I could speak all the languages of earth and of angels, but didn't love others, I would only be a noisy gong or a clanging cymbal"* (1 Corinthians 13:1).

> *Love is the key to effectiveness in your assignment—*
> *before any spiritual action can take place.*

People want to know if you love them—before you get "all spiritual" with them. Before you prophesy about them, they want to know if you love them. If you don't love the person you are prophesying over, your prophecy won't be clean, it will be contaminated. You may have the gift of prophecy and the Lord may be using you, but if you don't love, your words may be tainted with bitterness or resentment or another unrighteous attitude.

First Corinthians 13 is well-known, and for good reason—it is the ultimate definition of love. I believe love is so important that we should take an in-depth look into the kind of love Christ has for us and we should have for others. Let's start with 1 Corinthians 13:4-7:

> *Love is **patient** and **kind**. Love is **not jealous or boastful or proud or rude**. It **does not demand its own way**. It is **not irritable**, and it **keeps no record of being wronged**. It **does not rejoice about injustice** but **rejoices whenever the truth wins out**. Love **never gives up, never loses faith**, is **always hopeful**, and **endures through every circumstance**.*

LOVE IS PATIENT AND KIND

Not many people I know, including me, are patient. We live in a right-now society with instant this and that. Can we honestly say that we don't mind waiting for our turn in line at the coffee shop, at the bank, or even to greet the pastor on the way out of church? I would venture to say that we are impatient by nature. Even way back in biblical times people were impatient. Sarah, Abraham's wife, comes to my mind. Yours too? (See Genesis 16:1-4.)

What can we do to become patient people—people willing to "be still" when need be. I've heard it said that Christians shouldn't pray for patience because God will allow unfortunate circumstances to teach us that lesson. I tend to disagree. God's nature is love and He will help us become the people He wants us to be, not by harshness but by gentleness and kindness.

Have faith that you can be patient in every situation—if you focus on God and His "big picture." For example, maybe sitting in rush-hour traffic makes you angry. You sit there and stew about all the things you could be doing—but there you are moving along at 5-10 miles an hour. Rather than feeling your blood pressure rising, take some deep breaths and with each one thank God for the car you are in, for the gas in the tank, for the job you are going to or the home you are returning to. Focus on all the good things you have been blessed with—after all, God is the giver of all good things in your life (see Romans 8:28).

When your mind and spirit are concentrating on God's blessings, the natural response is one of kindness. Kindness toward those who may be in the car with you, kindness toward the driver who is trying to merge into your lane in front of you, kindness in your response to the construction workers alongside the dangerous roadway.

Jesus showed kindness to people every day during His ministry. He didn't turn away, shun, or ignore the poor, the unclean, the hungry, the hurting. When He saw that His Temple was being used inappropriately, He immediately restored it to the "house of prayer" it was meant to be and in kindness healed the blind and lame who came to Him (see Matthew 21:12-14).

Kindness comes naturally when we are walking in God's will for us—which is to become more like Jesus. When we take our cues from our Savior, we will always be patient and kind.

LOVE IS *NOT* JEALOUS, BOASTFUL, PROUD, RUDE

Paul tells us what love *is* and what it is *not*. When you read the words jealous, boastful, proud, and rude, do you immediately think of yourself—or someone else? Does a sibling, a parent, a co-worker, or maybe a spouse come to mind? All people have these tendencies, no one is exempt from these flaws in our character. We must recognize and work to eliminate these traits in ourselves, then others will notice and hopefully will want to emulate us. Entire books could be (and have been) written just on the topics of jealousy and pride. And no doubt we could have a lengthy discussion about the arrogant and impolite people we know. But that won't solve the problem.

To turn over the "Temple tables" of these unrighteous tendencies and attitudes, we must *love*. Love is the antidote for all attitudes that do not align with what we know to be true and right. When we covet someone's car or house or good grades or promotion, we are not loving that person. When we brag about our accomplishments and "things," we are not loving the person hearing us boast. When we take credit for God-given gifts, we are not loving the One who blessed us. And when we are ill-mannered, rude, and impolite, we are not conveying the love God has for people; in fact, we are portraying the opposite of His loving nature.

For God so loved the world that He gave His only begotten Son, that whoever believes in Him should not perish but have everlasting life (John 3:16 NKJV).

When we think about the most loving gift God could give to the world, we know the answer is Jesus, the ultimate Gift. The Gift who sacrificed Himself because He loves us—because His heavenly Father loves us. God is Love: *"anyone who does not love does not know God, for God is love"* (1 John 4:8).

Love Is *Not* Demanding, Irritable, Vengeful

Again, Paul mentions what love is *not,* because people can so easily fall into a habit of wanting their needs met above everyone else's. And when those needs aren't immediately satisfied, they become irritable and become vengeful. No one likes to be around irritable people. They are not pleasant, they find fault and bicker and are critical. They also hold grudges and keep track of those who wrong them—sometimes seriously plotting against them. And they are happy when things go wrong for the person. None of that is love—it is contrary to love.

Loving people actually demand nothing of others and are easy-going. They aren't vengeful and won't hold a grudge. Rather, they forgive and forget—modeling their Lord's mindset and nature.

Love Rejoices, Stays Strong, Is Hopeful and Enduring

Loving people rejoice when truth and righteousness prevail. Loving people persevere, they never give up or lose faith, they are hopeful and endure through every circumstance. That's a tall order to fill! How can Paul, speaking for God to the Corinthians, expect people to be like that? How? Because he knows that the Holy Spirit living within every believer will empower us to when the time comes.

Do you have a friend who rejoices with you when something great happens? Is there someone in your life you call right away when you get good news because you know he or she will be happy for you? We all need those types of friends—we all need to *be* that type of friend. If circumstances prevent you from having or being that type of person right now, maybe you moved to a different area or your job keeps you too busy to do much socializing, remember, Jesus will never leave you. He is your very best friend always. Your real and true BFF.

Staying strong, hopeful, and able to endure are traits that will serve you well throughout your life. The devil, the evil one, preys on weak people—people who don't know the power and strength they have by reading and knowing God's Word and leaning on the Holy Spirit. You have no reason to fear evil spirits or evil people—God is greater than anything the world can throw at you (see 1 John 4:4).

Hopeful people see the best in situations and people. Those who have hope have joy, as it is a by-product of seeing the good side, the silver lining. Consequently, joyful people can endure troubles and challenges because they have hope that they can and will endure. Consider seriously the words of James:

> *Dear brothers and sisters, when troubles of any kind come your way, consider it an opportunity for great joy. For you know that when your faith is tested, your endurance has a chance to grow. So let it grow, for when your endurance is fully developed, you will be perfect and complete, needing nothing. If you need wisdom, ask our generous God, and he will give it to you. He will not rebuke you for asking* (James 1:2-5).

"...you will be perfect and complete, needing nothing"—wow, isn't that a wonderful truth to accept! How can we doubt God when He tells us over and over through the Bible how much He loves us. Rather than imperfect people who mumble and grumble about troubles, we are to consider those times as opportunities for *"great joy"*! Of course that goes against our selfish nature—we instead tend to wallow in self-pity or whine to others about our misfortune. This should not be so. Read James 1:2-5 again, slowly and seriously. Absorb the truth into your being. It will do you well to reflect on this fact in times to come.

LOVE AND TRUST

I was in a meeting with my trustee board and one of the trustees mentioned this quote: "Love is resilient, but trust is fragile," which I think speaks volumes about personal relationships. For example, you may love your mother and father, but if one or both does or says something to strain or break your trust in them, the relationship may never be the same again—unless you determine to truly love them.

The experiences people go through in life can cause them to find it difficult to trust. When this happens it can also affect their relationship with God. As Christians, their relationships in general and even their relationship with their spiritual leader can falter, wither, even die. However, love is so powerful that it is the key to restoring healthy trust levels.

> **Trust** in the Lord with all your heart; do not depend on your own understanding. Seek his will in all you do, and he will show you which path to take (Proverbs 3:5-6).

Real Love Can Restore Trust

Some are afraid to trust God or others or even themselves. Fear is a terrible characteristic, it terrorizes emotions, attacks our physical well-being, and destroys relationships. A Scripture that comes to mind and demonstrates how powerful love is over fear is found in 1 John 4:18 (AMP):

> There is no fear in love [dread does not exist]. But **perfect (complete, full-grown) love drives out fear,** because fear involves [the expectation of divine] punishment, so the one who is afraid [of God's judgment] is not perfected in love [has not grown into a sufficient understanding of God's love].

Ungodly fear can be eliminated from your mind, spirit, and soul by—again—concentrating on God's goodness and His blessings in your life. Frightful fear can be destroyed by focusing on your assignment and accomplishing it. When you do, you are expanding the Kingdom of God, which enhances your inner and outer being, as well as those in your circle of influence.

The New International Version of Proverbs 1:7 tells us that, *"The fear of the Lord is the beginning of knowledge, but fools despise wisdom and instruction."* And the Amplified Bible expands the definition of godly fear:

The [reverent] fear of the Lord [that is, worshiping Him and regarding Him as truly awesome] is the beginning and the preeminent part of knowledge [its starting point and its essence]; but arrogant fools despise [skillful and godly] wisdom and instruction and self-discipline.

The "fear of the Lord" is totally different from the terrifying fear the evil one tries to conquer us with. We must know the difference and be ready to rid ourselves of the fear that immobilizes us from advancing the Kingdom of God.

You have probably read or heard it preached that the letters spelling FEAR can be thought of as False Evidence Appearing Real. Other notable quotes regarding fear have been uttered by famous and infamous people throughout the ages, including: "The only thing we have to fear is fear itself" by Franklin D. Roosevelt, US President.

The Bible is full of "Fear not" verses (about 100!), which tell us that fear is a natural reaction to situations that are strange or unfamiliar. Mary was told by an angel (Luke 1:30) to "Fear not"; likewise, the shepherds (Luke 2:10). Jesus told Simon (Luke 5:10) to fear not; and He was very specific about who to fear and not fear in His teaching about the fear of God in Luke 12:4-7 (NKJV):

And I say to you, My friends, do not be afraid of those who kill the body, and after that have no more that they can do. But I will show you whom you should fear: Fear Him who, after He has killed, has power to cast into hell; yes, I say to you, fear Him! "Are not five sparrows sold for two copper coins? And not one of them is forgotten before God. But the very hairs of your head are all numbered. **Do not fear** *therefore; you are of more value than many sparrows.*

Our heavenly Father is to be respected and worshipped and praised. He believes in us and has assigned us tasks that may scare us at times because we submit to the devil's tactics, including fear. The evil one knows that if we accomplish our assignment, God Almighty will give us another assignment—each one making us stronger, advancing His Kingdom on earth, and diminishing the devil's power over us.

To God only be the glory and power and the authority to reign in our hearts and minds and spirits.

CORPORATE LOVE

Not only do we have to personally and individually love others, we also as a universal Church need to love everyone who walks into our sanctuaries. Christians have not always been *inclusive*—rather we have been *exclusive,* sorting through the people who sit in the pews according to our prejudices and preferences.

We must accept each person who seeks God—no matter what they wear, their age, their hair style or color, the number of tattoos, or the color of their skin. With Jesus as our example of unconditional love, the corporate Church of God must welcome every seeker with open arms. It must become a lifestyle, a mindset, and a way of common practice.

Every believer has the assignment to love even the "unlovable," according to our standards. We are loveable, according to God's standards. Therefore, as Christians, followers of Christ, we should look for the good in people and help bring out their best qualities. This may take more than a once-a-month get-together or even a once-a-week lunch discussion. God's assignment for you may be to mentor or shepherd someone for multiple months or a year. Every soul saved and matured is a soul you will be singing with in Heaven for eternity. Hallelujah!

We can't throw away people. Each one is precious in God's sight—and should be in our sight. Now it's true that we need to be discerning and we can't take on someone who will drag us down. We must be in serious prayer about the difference between the two responsibilities.

TRUE LOVE VERSUS MOVIE LOVE

In your mind, think about the types of love you have encountered over the years. I venture to speculate that you are thinking about the love shown by a:

- Mother
- Husband
- Wife
- Child
- Family member

- Best friend

- Pastor

- Favorite teacher

This type of love is the love God infuses into our hearts. The type of love that tries to look for the good in the person, tries to forgive and forget when hurt or disappointed. Without the Holy Spirit living in us, it is hard to love even these special people in our lives when they frustrate or annoy us. When the God of love is guiding our motives and mouths, we become people who attract others. When people are attracted to us by our genuine love for them, they will be open and receptive to hear the Good News of the Gospel!

On the other hand, the type of so-called love that is portrayed in the movies and on television and on the Internet is the devil's hook, perverting what is wonderful and pure. When love is boiled down to only a sexual act, people are blinded and no good comes from it. And when love is portrayed as the desire for chocolate, an expensive car, the latest fashion, a new hair color, or a night on the town, people who know nothing of the true love of God are swindled by the evil intentions of the one who comes only to steal, kill, and destroy (see John 10:10).

Too often we are too weak to withstand the clever and cunning ways of the world, too easily taken in by the glam and glitz of the sales ads and the "easy payments" and the promises of beauty, love, and a better life. Our commercialized society's bottom line seems to be making the most amount of money in the least amount of time.

When we are anointed with the Spirit of the Lord, we are empowered to face and proclaim victory over what the slicksters offer. We are empowered to accept our assignments and fulfill them totally, making the world and those around us want what we have—a full and joyful life, peace that passes their understanding, and assurance of eternity in Heaven.

Chapter 3

THE PURPOSE OF
THE SPIRIT OF THE LORD

The Spirit of the Lord God is upon Me... (Isaiah 61:1 NKJV).

The Spirit of the Lord is upon Me... (Luke 4:18 NKJV).

Luke 4 tells us that Jesus read from Isaiah 61, declaring that the Spirit of the Lord God was upon Him as the Son of the Most High God. Jesus claimed as His own the words written in Isaiah 61. This was a monumental declaration, this was an unheard of proclamation from a guy whose father was a carpenter. Little did the people in the synagogue that day know that Jesus had just defeated the devil in the wilderness. He earned the right to make that claim of His deity—His sovereignty, because the Spirit of the Lord God was upon Him.

The Spirit of the Lord *empowers* us for the assignment given to us from before our very beginning. In other words, the Holy Spirit gives us power within to complete our assignment. The word "power" in the Greek is *dunamis,* which means force, miraculous power, ability, strength, and might.

Jesus was filled with the Holy Spirit and He healed the sick; He was empowered by the Spirit of the Lord to accomplish His God-given assignment. Empowered means we have inspiration, personal assistance, and power *(dunamis)* to complete the task. If Jesus needed to be empowered by God, certainly we must be empowered by the Holy Spirit to fulfill our assignments as well. We cannot love or heal or restore by our own flesh, by our own mental or physical capability, by our own knowledge or wisdom—no. We must be filled with the Holy Spirit's supernatural power, ability, strength, and might.

As mentioned in a previous chapter, God will not give you an assignment that you are not capable of achieving. He will prepare you in every way to successfully accomplish the tasks He assigns you. Micah 3:8 says, *"But as for me, I am filled with power—with the Spirit of the Lord. I am filled with justice and strength...."*

Acts 1:8 (AMP) tells us:

*You will receive **power and ability** when the Holy Spirit comes upon you; and you will be My witnesses [to tell people about Me] both in Jerusalem and in all Judea, and Samaria, and even to the ends of the earth.*

Not only will we receive the ability to share the Gospel—at home, work, church, the grocery store, in line at the movie theatre—but also the *power* to speak the truth. You will have the power to destroy the fear of rejection and the butterflies in your stomach and proclaim boldly God's plan for salvation.

The Spirit of the Lord empowers you!

The purpose of the Spirit of the Lord is also to empower us to see things never seen before, to open our eyes to the spiritual world. For example, Ezekiel 37:1-5,10 tells us:

*The Lord took hold of me, and I was carried away by the **Spirit of the Lord** to a valley filled with bones. He led me all around among the bones that covered the valley floor. They were scattered everywhere across the ground and were completely dried out. Then he asked me, "Son of man, can these bones become living people again?" "O Sovereign Lord," I replied, "you alone know the answer to that." Then he said to me, "Speak a prophetic message to these bones and say, 'Dry bones, listen to the word of the Lord! This is what the Sovereign Lord says: Look! I am going to put breath into you and make you live again! ...So I spoke the message as he commanded me, and breath* *came into their bodies. They all came to life and stood up on their feet—a great army.*

Caleb and Joshua saw with their spiritual eyes a land of abundance, easy to take for the Israelites' own. Others saw a land filled with giants, refusing to see God's reality. Caleb and Joshua passed the test and were rewarded with entry into the land (see Numbers 13:30-33; 14:36-38). There are numerous other such stories throughout the Bible—I encourage you to read them and to ask God to open your eyes to the spiritual world where He will show you amazing and wonderful things.

The Holy Spirit will allow us to be placed in vulnerable situations where we will be tested. The result of our times of testing will qualify us for our assignments. Even Jesus was tested—the Son of the Almighty God was tested. Matthew 4:1 (AMP) says, *"Then Jesus was led by the [Holy] Spirit into the wilderness to be tempted by the devil."* Mark's Gospel says, *"The Spirit then compelled Jesus to go into the wilderness, where he was tempted by Satan for forty days."* At times you will be led into situations so God can qualify you—you aren't qualified to accomplish your assignment until you pass the test. You may have lived through hell last year or last month, but now you are qualified for your assignment—and the evil one can't disqualify you.

So we should also expect God to relocate us and show us things through the Spirit—things that our naked eyes cannot see or comprehend. The Holy Spirit will lead and guide us and bring things to our remembrance. Jesus tells His disciples in John 14:26 (NKJV) that:

> *The Helper, the Holy Spirit, whom the Father will send in My name, He will teach you all things, and bring to your remembrance all things that I said to you.*

The Spirit of the Lord lives within us. When Jesus ascended into Heaven, after completing His assignment on earth, He didn't leave us totally alone. No. The Father sent the Holy Spirit to dwell with and in us—to guide us and remind us of Jesus's teachings. Paul wrote to the church in Corinth saying: *"Do you not know that you are the temple of God and that the Spirit of God dwells in you?"*

The Spirit of the Lord lives within you.

The Holy Spirit, the Spirit of the Lord, is part of the Triune God: Father, Son, and Holy Spirit—Three in One. The Bible mentions the Holy Spirit more than 100 times. He is as important as God the Father and Jesus the Son. Paul extensively refers to the power of the Holy Spirit in his life and in the life of every believer. His send-off in 2 Corinthians 13:14 is well-known: *"The grace of the Lord Jesus Christ, and the love of God, and the communion of the Holy Spirit be with you all."*

Well-known gospel singer Fred Hammond is known as a gifted songwriter, bassist, and vocalist. I'd like to share portions of lyrics from his song, *When the Spirit of the Lord:*

> *When the Spirit of the Lord comes upon my heart*
> *I will dance like David danced.*
>
> *When the Spirit of the Lord comes upon my heart*
> *I will pray like David prayed.*
>
> *When the Spirit of the Lord comes upon my heart*
> *I will sing like David sang.*

David was anointed by Samuel and the Spirit of the Lord came upon David from that day forward (see 1 Samuel 16:13). Yes, like David, when the Spirit of the Lord fills us, we will feel like dancing and praying and singing, and sometimes even:

- going to war[1]
- blowing the trumpet of victory[2]
- tearing a lion apart[3]
- breaking loose from bondage[4]
- prophesying[5]
- defying time and space[6]
- declaring liberty[7]
- and performing amazing feats for His glory

God gives us His Spirit as a gift—a gift of love and grace and mercy to help others and ourselves become the people He intended us to be. According to world-renown evangelist Billy Graham, one of the assignments of the Holy Spirit is to:

> convict us of our sin. Jesus said, "And when He has come, He will convict the world of sin, and of righteousness, and of judgment" (John 16:8). The Holy Spirit uses a mother's prayers, a tragic experience, a pastor's sermon or some other experience to convict us of sin and of our need to turn our lives over to Jesus Christ. He points to us and says, "You are a sinner. You need to repent." We don't like to hear that, but that is the work of the Holy Spirit. Without that work we could never have our sins forgiven. We could never be saved. We could never go to Heaven.[8]

When the Spirit of the Lord comes to live in our hearts, we are supernaturally empowered. This power is universal yet different for each person and for each instance needed. The power we receive for a task today may not be the same power we receive next week for our next assignment. Solomon received wisdom power; Samson received physical power; Joseph received compassionate power, John the Baptist received proclaiming power, John the Revelator received revelation power. Throughout the Bible there are many, many stories about men and women receiving power, strength, wisdom, and compassion at the moment they needed it.

Jesus received from the Spirit of the Lord the power He needed to endure and overcome the evil and disappointments and challenges He encountered here on earth at the hands of critics and betrayers. Ultimately, Jesus received the Spirit of Life eternal and sits at the right hand of God Almighty, judging the living and the dead—now and forevermore.

Paul said to Titus, "[God] *saved us, not because of the righteous things we had done, but because of his mercy. He washed away our sins, giving us a new birth and new life through the Holy Spirit"* (Titus 3:5).

Charles Haddon Spurgeon, the great pastor in England during the 1800s, delivered a sermon based on 2 Corinthians 3:17 that is most relevant for us today. I believe so relevant and important that I am going to share excerpts with you now. (Please realize that Pastor Spurgeon was speaking about women too. In no way does he—nor do I—exclude women from all that God has for all of His children—men and women alike.)

Liberty is the birthright of every man. He may be born a pauper; he may be a foundling; his parentage may be altogether unknown; but liberty is his inalienable birthright. Black may be his skin; he may live uneducated and untaught; he may be poor as poverty itself; he may never have a foot of land to call his own; he may scarce have a particle of clothing, save a few rags to cover him; but, poor as he is, nature has fashioned him for freedom— he has a right to be free, and if he has not liberty, it is his birthright, and he ought not to be content until he wins it.

Liberty is the heirloom of all the sons and daughters of Adam. But where do you find liberty unaccompanied by religion? True it is that all men have a right to liberty, but it is equally true that you do not meet it in any country save where you find the Spirit of the Lord. "Where the Spirit of the Lord is, there is liberty." Thank God, this is a free country. This is a land where I can breathe the air and say it is untainted by the groan of a single slave; my lungs receive it, and I know there has never been mingled with its vapours the tear of a single slave woman shed over her child which has been sold from her. This land is the home of liberty. But why is it so? I take it, it is not so much because of our institutions as because the Spirit of the Lord is here—the spirit of true and hearty religion.

There was a time, remember, when England was no more free than any other country, when men could not speak their sentiments freely, when kings were despots, when Parliaments were but a name. Who won our liberties for us? Who have loosed our chains? Under the hand of God, I say, the men of religion—men like the great and glorious Cromwell, who would have liberty of conscience, or die—men who, if they could not reach kings' hearts, because they were unsearchable in cunning, would strike kings low, rather than they would be slaves.

We owe our liberty to men of religion, to men of the stern Puritanical school—men who scorned to play the craven and yield their principles at the command of man. And if we ever are to maintain our liberty (as God grant we may) it shall be kept in England by religious liberty—by religion. This Bible is the Magna Charta of old Britain. Its truths, its doctrines have snapped our fetters, and they never can be riveted on again, whilst men, with God's Spirit in their hearts, go forth to speak its truths. In no other land, save where the Bible is unclasped—in no other realm, save where the gospel is preached, can you find liberty. Roam through other countries, and you speak with bated breath; you are afraid; you feel you are under an iron hand; the sword is above you; you are not free. Why? Because you are under the tyranny engendered by a false religion: you have not free Protestantism there; and it is not till Protestantism comes that there can be freedom. It is where the Spirit of the Lord is that there is liberty, and nowhere else. Men talk about being free: they describe model governments, Platonic republics, or Owenite paradises; but they are dreamy theorists; for there can be no freedom in the world, save, "where the spirit of the Lord is."

I have commenced with this idea, because I think worldly men ought to be told that if religion does not save them, yet it has done much for them—that the influence of religion has won them their liberties.

But the liberty of the text is no such freedom as this: it is an infinitely greater and better one. Great as civil or religious liberty may be, the liberty of my text transcendently exceeds. There is a liberty, dear friends, which Christian men alone enjoy; for even in Great Britain there are men who taste not the sweet air of liberty. There are some who are afraid to speak as men, who have to cringe and fawn, and bow, and stoop, to any one; who have no will of their own, no principles, no voice, no courage, and who cannot stand erect in conscious independence. But he is the free man, whom the truth makes free. He who has grace in his heart is free; he cares for no one; he has the right upon his side; he has God within him—the indwelling Spirit of the Holy Ghost; he is a prince of the blood royal of heaven; he is a noble, having the true patent of nobility; he is one of God's elect, distinguished, chosen children, and he is not the man to bend, or meanly cringe. No!—sooner would he walk the burning furnace with Shadrach, Meshach, and Abednego—sooner would he be cast into the lion's den with Daniel, than yield a point of principle. He is a free man.

"Where the Spirit of the Lord is, there is liberty" in its fullest, highest, and widest sense. God gives you friends, to have that "Spirit of the Lord;" for without it, in a free country, ye may still be bondsmen; and where there are no serfs in body, ye may be slaves in soul. The text speaks of Spiritual liberty; and now I address the children of God. Spiritual liberty, brethren, you and I enjoy if we have "the Spirit of the Lord" within us. What does this imply? It implies that there was a time when we had not that Spiritual liberty—when we were slaves. But a little while ago all of us who now are free in Christ Jesus, were slaves of the devil: we were led captives at his will. We talked of free-will, but free will is a slave. We boasted that we could do what we pleased; but oh! what a slavish and dreamy liberty we had. It was a fancied freedom. We were slaves to our lusts and passions—slaves to sin; but now we are freed from sin; we are delivered from our tyrant; a stronger than he has cast out the strong man armed, and we are free.

..."Where the Spirit of the Lord is, there is liberty" in all holy acts of *love—liberty from a slavish fear of law*. Many people are honest because they are afraid of the policeman. Many are sober because they are afraid of the eye of the public. Many persons are seemingly religious because of their neighbours. There is much virtue which is like the juice of the grape—it has to be squeezed before you get it; it is not like the generous drop of the honeycomb, distilling willingly and freely. I am bold to say, that if a man be destitute of the grace of God, his works are only works of slavery; he feels forced to do them.

I know before I came into the liberty of the children of God, if I went to God's house, I went because I thought I must do it; if I prayed, it was because I feared some misfortune would happen in the day if I did not; if I ever thanked God for mercy, it was because I thought I should not get another if I were not thankful; if I performed a righteous deed, it was with the hope that very likely God would reward me at last, and I should be winning some crown in heaven. A poor slave, a mere Gibeonite, hewing wood and drawing water. If I could have left off doing it, I should have loved to do so. If I could have had my will, there would have been no chapel-going for me, no religion for me—I would have lived in the world and followed the ways of Satan, if I could have done as I pleased. As for righteousness, it was slavery; sin would have been my liberty.

But now, Christian, what is your liberty? What makes you come to the house of God to day?

> *"Love made your willing feet*
> *In swift obedience move."*

What makes you bend your knee in prayer? It is because you like to talk with your Father who seeth in secret. What is it that opens your purses, and makes you give liberally? It is because you love the poor children of God, and you feel, so much being given to you, that it is a privilege to give something back to Christ. What is it that constrains you to live honestly, righteously, and soberly? Is it the rear of the jail? No; you might pull the jail down; you might annihilate the convict settlements; you might hurl all chains into the sea; and we should be just as holy as we are now.

Some people say, "Then, sir, you mean to say that Christians may live as they like." I wish they could, sir. If I could live as I liked, I would, always live holily. If a Christian could live as he liked, he would always live as he ought. It is a slavery to him to sin; righteousness is his delight. Oh! if I could but live as I list, I would list to live as I ought. If I could but live as I would I would live as God commands me.

The greatest happiness of a Christian is to be holy. It is no slavery to him. Put him where you will, he will not sin, Expose him to any temptation, if it were not for that evil heart still remaining, you would never find him sinning. Holiness is his pleasure; sin is his slavery. Ah! ye poor bondsmen who come to church and chapel because ye must; ah! ye poor slavish moralists that are honest because of the gyves, and sober because of the prison; ah! ye poor slaves! We are not so; we are not under the law, but under grace.[9]

Although spoken more than 150 years ago, the words could not be any more true. Baptist preacher Charles Haddon Spurgeon was England's best-known preacher for most of the second half of the 19th century. He frequently preached to audiences of more than 10,000 people. Spurgeon continues to be quoted by pastors, teachers, secular and spiritual people in books, magazine articles, and on the Internet.

Did Pastor Spurgeon accomplish his God-given assignment? Yes, I believe he did. He was filled with the Spirit of the Lord and used that power and insights from God to share the Gospel with millions of people in his time—and the centuries that followed.

As mentioned previously, not all of us are called to preach in front of thousands, hundreds, or even in a small group. But we all are called to share the Gospel with the one to whom God leads us. When you feel the still, small voice rise up within you when you are having lunch with an unbeliever, working side by side with a neighbor, standing in line at the market, follow the Voice's lead. Gently and sincerely share the hope and love you have as the Spirit of the Lord gives you the words. The more you step out in faith, the easier it will become.

ENDNOTES

1. Judges 3:10.
2. Judges 6:34.
3. Judges 14:6.
4. Judges 15:14.
5. 1 Samuel 10:6.

6. Acts 8:39.

7. 2 Corinthians 3:17.

8. Billy Graham, April 30, 2009; http://billygraham.org/decision-magazine/may-2009/ does-the-holy-spirit-live-in-you/; accessed January 18, 2016.

9. Rev. C. H. Spurgeon, *The New Park Street Pulpit,* "Spiritual Liberty," February 18, 1855, Exeter Hall, Strand., England; http://spurgeon.org/sermons/0009.htm; accessed January 18, 2016.

Chapter 4

ARE YOU ANOINTED?

*The Spirit of the Sovereign Lord is upon me, for **the Lord has anointed me**...* (Isaiah 61:1).

The title of this chapter asks a question. Are you anointed? Are you? Think about it for a moment or two. What does being anointed mean to you? Should you want to be anointed? Is everyone anointed? These questions are important and need to be answered as part of understanding your God-given assignment. As the Bible states, Christians need to go beyond being fed milk, we need to mature into meat-eaters, devouring all that the Word has to give us for full spiritual nourishment.

The answer to the first question—are you anointed—is yes! Yes, you are anointed if you are a born-again believer who trusts in the Lord to use you to advance His Kingdom here on earth and to bring you to Himself when your assignment here is completed. Yes, you are anointed for the assignment that God has given you. And you are not just anointed as a cool thing to be or say or as a status symbol or something to boast about to others. There is a *purpose* to your anointing. You are anointed so you can do, say, and think according to God's will and fulfill your assignment as the anointing enables you to do so.

Jesus read about Himself in Isaiah 61:1, "*...Because the Lord has anointed Me....*" Jesus knew He was anointed, He knew He had an assignment from God that would change the world forever. He took His assignment seriously from the moment He began His ministry; He ate, slept, preached, healed, loved, and felt it throughout His being 24-7.

Each of us has a particular, unique assignment. Jesus had His—I have mine— you have yours. And when we are anointed with the Spirit of the Lord, no one can stop us! People will have to get out of our way because we are marching through life with power and might! All enemy strongholds will be destroyed—we will have breakthrough after breakthrough on our way to completing our assignments. The devil will not be able to stop us, our nemesis at work or even at church will not be able to stop us. We are unstoppable when we realize who we are as God's anointed, chosen people.

You are unstoppable!

The word "anoint" means to rub on; apply an ointment, or oily liquid to a person or a thing. The Hebrew word for "anoint" is *mashiah,* which comes to us as "messiah." It is translated as *christos* in Greek. Because we now use this term exclusively for Jesus Christ, the Messiah, many have failed to realize the breadth of its meaning. *Mashiah* simply means anointed, or "anointed one." The word "Christ" is not Jesus's last name. Jesus Christ means Jesus the Anointed—He had an assignment.

Contrary to what many believe, the anointing is not being "slain in the spirit," jumping up and down, speaking in tongues, etc. These are various physical *expressions* that people exhibit when they experience or feel moved by the Holy Spirit. These expressions should not be confused with what the Scriptures describe as a spiritual anointing.

The Old Testament writers use *mashiah* and its verb form, *mashah,* to describe prophets, kings, and priests. Normally, these people were anointed with oil in a ritual as a sign of being set apart for the office that they were about to fulfill. Thus, at its most basic definition, *mashiah* indicates a person God authorizes and sets apart for His service. Persons in the Old Testament were often physically anointed with oil. For example, priests were anointed for their special service to the Lord (see Exodus 28:41). In this ritual, oil would be applied to the person's head as a sign upon their lives for service (see Exodus 29:7). Scriptures refer to this as an anointing from the Holy One (see 1 John 2:20 NKJV).

Isaiah prophetically speaks of the Messiah; and in Luke, the Messiah (Jesus Christ) announces that He is empowered by the Spirit of the Lord God for His assignment (Luke 4:18,21).

When people say that someone is "anointed," it means that person is walking strongly in his or her assignment. When we say we "see the anointing" on a person, we are actually seeing someone carrying out his or her assignment. As revealed throughout the Bible, Jesus's life reflects His concentrated focus on His assignment. Every decision and movement and thought was based on advancing toward the completion of His assignment.

Even at an early age Jesus knew His assignment and walked in it:

> *So when they* [Jesus's parents] *did not find Him, they returned to Jerusalem, seeking Him. Now so it was that after three days they found Him in the temple, sitting in the midst of the teachers, both listening to them and asking them questions. And all who heard Him were astonished at His understanding and answers. So when they saw Him, they were amazed; and His mother said to Him, "Son, why have You done this to us? Look, Your father and I have sought You anxiously." And He said to them, "Why did you seek Me? Did you not know that I must be about My Father's business?"* (Luke 2:45-49 NKJV)

Likewise, we must walk in our anointing, our assignment from sunup to sundown. We are to focus on God's will in our lives, which will bring us peace and joy and unfailing love from Him.

Back in the day, in the Old Testament, the Lord spoke, and the people took the anointing literally and practiced it physically. God spoke to Moses about the specific ingredients to be used to make the anointing oil:

> *Moreover the Lord spoke to Moses, saying: "Also take for yourself **quality spices**—five hundred shekels of liquid myrrh, half as much sweet-smelling cinnamon (two hundred and fifty shekels), two hundred and fifty shekels of sweet-smelling cane, five hundred shekels of cassia, according to the shekel of the sanctuary, and a hin of **olive oil**. And you shall **make from these a holy anointing oil**, an ointment compounded according to the art of the perfumer. It shall be **a holy anointing oil**. With it you shall anoint the tab-*

*ernacle of meeting and the ark of the Testimony; the table and all its utensils, the lampstand and its utensils, and the altar of incense; the altar of burnt offering with all its utensils, and the laver and its base. You shall consecrate them, that they may be most holy; whatever touches them must be holy. And you shall **anoint Aaron and his sons**, and consecrate them, that they may minister to Me as priests"* (Exodus 30:22-30 NKJV).

What was anointed with the oil was consecrated for God's use. The tabernacle, the ark, the table and utensils, the lampstand and utensils, the altars—and Aaron and his sons, so they can fulfill their assignments as priests.

The anointing was and is a serious matter for us to consider. In God's eyes, the anointing is an important aspect in our quest to obey His directives. Jesus scolded His disciples when they disapproved of the woman who anointed Him with oil. In fact, He told them that her action would be remembered and discussed throughout the world. And here you are reading about her centuries later in a land very far away from where it happened:

*Meanwhile, Jesus was in Bethany at the home of Simon, a man who had previously had leprosy. While he was eating, a woman came in with a beautiful alabaster jar of expensive perfume made from essence of nard. **She broke open the jar and poured the perfume over his head.** Some of those at the table were indignant. "Why waste such expensive perfume?" they asked. "It could have been sold for a year's wages and the money given to the poor!" So they scolded her harshly. But Jesus replied, "Leave her alone. Why criticize her for doing such a good thing to me? You will always have the poor among you, and you can help them whenever you want to. But you will not always have me. **She** has done what she could and **has anointed my body for burial ahead of time.** I tell you the truth, wherever the Good News is preached throughout the world, this woman's deed will be remembered and discussed"* (Mark 14:3-9).

Although Jesus was filled with the Spirit of the Lord and the Holy Spirit lived within Him throughout His life on earth, the anointing He received empowered Him to carry out His assignment; and this last outward anointing with oil was symbolic of the spiritual anointing He had received when the dove descended from Heaven the day He was baptized by John:

> *When all the people were baptized, it came to pass that Jesus also was baptized; and while He prayed, the heaven was opened. And the Holy Spirit descended in bodily form like a dove upon Him, and a voice came from heaven which said, "You are My beloved Son; in You I am well pleased"* (Luke 3:21-22 NKJV).

We can be assured that the Holy Spirit will descend upon us too, as we are truly obedient and faithful to God's will for our lives. We too can hear God say He is well-pleased with us when the time comes.

Of course the Old Testament cites often the use of anointing oil; but this ritual is not restricted to ancient times. Some modern-day churches and ministries have eliminated anointing people with oil—others make it a routine part of weekly services. In the New Testament, James tells us to bring to church anyone who is sick and *"pray over you, anointing you with oil in the name of the Lord"* (James 5:14); and Mark tells us how Jesus's disciples *"anointed with oil many who were sick, and healed them"* (Mark 6:13 NKJV).

Thousands have witnessed healings by men and women throughout modern times—by anointed healers such as John G. Lake, Smith Wigglesworth, Aimee Semple McPherson, Oral Roberts, William Branham, and Kathryn Kuhlman to name a few. A Catholic priest, Father Richard McAlear, has been healing people for more than 40 years, although he doesn't claim to have the gift of healing, only the gift of prayer, saying, "We pray to God and things happen. I know it's not me; I know God is there, and I'm almost watching Him do things. It's Jesus' compassion, the love of God that is doing the healing."[1]

"Snake Oil"

Don't be taken in by the devil's clever ruses meant to trivialize the holiness of the anointing and subsequently the anointing oil. We know that the evil one uses entrapments that are so similar to the real, holy words and aspects of God's spiritual realm that even true believers can be fooled. For instance, how the serpent so twisted God's words to Adam and Eve that they were deceived—these two perfectly created human beings who walked daily side by side with God Almighty! How much more so do we need to be on guard against his wiles.

An Internet search of the words "anointing oil" resulted in more than 1 million Websites. Some referred to actual oils for purchase and others were definitions of anointing oil or books supposedly revealing the mysterious oil and its supernatural capacity. One pastor explained that "when you pray over a bottle of natural olive oil in Jesus's name, God sets it apart and it becomes holy anointing oil. Use the oil for God's glory and see His miracles, prosperity and restoration in your life!"[2] Depending on the sincerity of the person praying and God's will for that individual, this may or may not ring true. We must never put our faith in a "thing" when we have Jesus, God's own Son, in whom to place our trust and faith.

One Website offered more than twenty "anointing oils" ranging from $4.99 to $33.99 and including:

Cedar of Lebanon

Pomegranate

Balm of Gilead

Frankincense & Myrrh

Prayer of Faith

Lily of the Valley

Rose of Sharon

Latter Rain

Spikenard

There were also assortments of vials to hold the oil, including those of "various colors" and sizes and prices. I doubt the Lord had mass-produced, commercialized anointing oil in mind when He told Moses how to make the oil He required back then. But we do know *that God causes everything to work together for the good of those who love God and are called according to his purpose for them*" (Romans 8:28).

We must turn to the Lord only for healing—physical, spiritual, emotional, mental, relational. Be wise and discerning when seeking the anointing; God's servants will be genuine and you will know in your spirit those in whom you can trust. Pray always for the Holy Spirit to open your spiritual eyes to the motives and intentions.

PRAY FOR THE ANOINTING

I found the following "Prayer for Anointing" in the *Tozer Devotional*[3] very poignant regarding asking to be anointed. The prayer is very specific and bodes well for us to compose a similar prayer when we feel the pressures of the world closing in on us.

> It is time, O God, for Thee to work, for the enemy has entered into Thy pasture, and the sheep are torn and scattered. False shepherds abound who deny the danger and laugh at the perils, which surround Thy flock. Lord Jesus, I come to Thee for spiritual preparation. Lay Thy hand upon me; anoint me with the oil of the New Testament prophet. Save me from the error of judging a church by its size, its popularity, or the amount of its yearly offering. Help me to remember that I am a prophet, not a promoter, not a religious manager. Let me never become a slave to crowds. Heal my soul of carnal ambitions and deliver me from the itch for publicity. Lay Thy terror upon me, O God, and drive me to the place of prayer, where I may wrestle with principalities and powers and the rulers of the darkness of this world. Teach me self-discipline, that I may be a good soldier of Jesus Christ.

The writer asks to be anointed with the oil of the New Testament prophet, which is an especially interesting phrase and request. The New Testament is all about Jesus—and His complete submission to His heavenly Father's will. When we can surrender all, we can defeat all the works of the devil.

How specific are you when you pray? This prayer is unlike many prayers we hear and read today. It's genuine, heart-felt and precise. Obviously the pray-er (person praying) has been faced with these troubles and temptations and is coming to the Lord "for spiritual preparation." We all face challenges, and God knows all about them. But that doesn't mean He won't listen intently when we ask Him to save us from ourselves, from the devil, from others meaning us harm.

Yes, we are anointed the moment we accept Jesus as our Lord and Savior, but remembering, acknowledging, and asking for His anointing is acceptable. Our heavenly Father appreciates that we desire more from Him, to be closer to Him, to absorb all that He has for us—daily, hourly, moment-by-moment.

Have you been anointed with oil in your local church or home group? Were you anointed for healing? Or to be set apart for a certain ministry or service? Why did you feel it necessary to receive the anointing with oil? How did it make you feel? These are important questions only you can answer with the assistance of the Holy Spirit. You may be surprised at your answers once you take the time to consider each.

I like the way the Amplified Bible expands the truth about the anointing in 1 John 2:27:

As for you, the anointing [the special gift, the preparation] which you received from Him remains [permanently] in you, and you have no need for anyone to teach you. But just as His anointing teaches you [giving you insight through the presence of the Holy Spirit] about all things, and is true and is not a lie, and just as His anointing has taught you, you must remain in Him [being rooted in Him, knit to Him].

From this Scripture passage we know that the anointing is a special gift to prepare us for and carry us through our assignment successfully. We have no need of someone else's guidance, because the God of all wisdom resides in us permanently. But...we must continue to accept His insights, trust in His presence, and obey His teachings. We must do our part to remain faithful.

God is a good God—He will not forsake us. We oftentimes forsake Him, unfortunately. He relentlessly remains with us; we are the ones who move away from Him—seeking fame or fortune or love in the wrong places and people. In the very beginning, God gave Adam and Eve all they needed, the very essence of love and beauty. But that wasn't enough. How many times did the Israelites forsake their eternal, unconditional-loving Almighty God for temporary, conditional-loving people, things, and places? It's never enough; we are never satisfied.

When that realization hits us, only then will we know that God is the only way to a life full of love and abundant blessings—of genuine satisfaction within our hearts, minds, and spirits. God is the only Source of contentment—of good tidings of great joy!

ENDNOTES

1. Sonja Corbitt, "The Finger of God for Healing: Faith Healing Priest Draws Thousands," Catholic Online, 5/28/2010; http://www.catholic.org/news/hf/faith/story.php?id=36722; accessed January 21, 2016.

2. Joseph Prince, "Understanding the Significance of the Olive Tree and Anointing Oil," August 2010; Gospel Revolution Vol. 3 Issue 3; http://www.josephprince.org/daily-grace/articles/single/understanding-the-significance-of-the-olive-tree-and-anointing-oil/; accessed January 18, 2016.

3. "Prayer for Anointing," *Tozer Devotional,* August 24, 2015; http://www.cmalliance.org/devotions/tozer?id=182; accessed January 18, 2016.

Chapter 5

SHARING GOOD TIDINGS

*The Spirit of the Sovereign Lord is upon me, for **the Lord has anointed me to bring good news to the poor**... (Isaiah 61:1).*

We are to especially share God's good tidings—the Good News of the Gospel—to poor, distressed, and impoverished people. Our message must bring hope to those who are hurting, suffering, and feeling abandoned. They enter church doors or they sit beside you on the bus or they are in line with you at the market—hurting people are all around us. We need to give them hope. Each of us individually and the Body of Christ corporately need to reach out with hope. Hope gives life and is a promise of a better life.

As modern-day Christians with access to the world through the Internet, we can reach out and actually communicate with people thousands of miles away in far-off continents, as well as connect with a neighbor down the street whom we have never met. We have the great opportunity—and responsibility—to encourage others, to give them hope, to make them smile, to bring brightness into their dark and dreary world by sharing the Good News of salvation.

There are more lonely and sad people than we can even imagine, right around the corner, right upstairs, right in the next cubicle, right...where you are.

Today we can reach out with a phone call, a text, an email, a tweet, a letter or postcard (remember those?). And, of course, we can be one of the 1.4 *billion* people who have joined Facebook. But please be careful who you choose as a "friend." And be careful, too, what comments you "like" if the posts are foolishness—if the person is only tearing others down or speaking gossip or lies about others. If we condone such social media talk, we can quickly give our "friends" the wrong impression of Christianity. Christians are held to a high standard by our righteous heavenly Father. We are to be His public relations people—showing the world through our words and actions all the good and love available to them.

So be careful what you post on social media, don't write anything that can distract or dissuade someone from receiving the true message of hope that Christ came to bring. If what we post is unrighteous, whoever reads it may think, "If that is Christianity, why should I follow it?!" Someone put this comment up on social media and I liked it so much that I reposted it—and share it with you now: "Make a habit of shutting down conversations that aim to tear others down."

I encourage you to "unfollow" or "unfriend" anyone who posts any type of stupidity or negativity. Yes, that may mean deleting quite a few people, but you will gain peace of mind and a purer heart if you allow only positive and hopeful people and communication into your life. You will feel the difference right away! We are to follow Christ—not "follow" people who are dragging us down, or others down.

Scripture warns us to be careful about what we say and do as Christians. Note the words in 1 Corinthians 8:9 (NKJV), *"But beware lest somehow this liberty of yours become a stumbling block to those who are weak."* Also consider the words in Galatians 5:13-14:

For you have been called to live in freedom, my brothers and sisters. But don't use your freedom to satisfy your sinful nature. Instead, use your freedom to serve one another in love. For the whole law can be summed up in this one command: "Love your neighbor as yourself."

So if what you are saying in person or on social media has no love in it—you should not be saying it.

If what you are saying has no love in it—you should not be saying it.

I've had to call people and tell them to take down their post—take it off their site. There can be no foolishness by Christians who are following Christ. We must realize that others will be affected by what we post, what we say, what we do.

We are supposed to preach good tidings! We are not supposed to preach anger or bitterness or fear or folly. No. We are to share the *good* news—*good* tidings. Going back to Isaiah again, he says in chapter 52:

> ***How beautiful*** *on the mountains are the feet of those who* ***bring good news,*** *who* ***proclaim peace,*** *who* ***bring good tidings,*** *who* ***proclaim salvation,*** *who say to Zion, "Your* ***God reigns!"*** (Isaiah 52:7 NIV)

We are elevated to the mountaintop and considered beautiful as we bring the good news to others. It brightens our day when we are given a sincere compliment, told we are appreciated, and asked for our advice. Likewise, when you give someone a genuine compliment, tell someone how much you appreciate him or her, and when you ask a trusted, wise person for advice, you are bringing them good tidings that will make a positive difference in their day—perhaps it will carry over into the rest of their lives.

For example, if you tell a youngster that he or she has a special talent for math or writing, that young person may take your comment seriously and begin to focus on cultivating that skill. Or if you tell a teenager how impressed you are with her or his public speaking ability, you may just nudge that teen to pursue a career that requires that skill.

Glad tidings are happy, pleasant comments that
enhance a person's outlook.

Glad tidings are happy, pleasant statements that enhance a person's outlook. The word "glad" means to be pleased, delighted, happy, overjoyed, thrilled, and the like. Who doesn't want to be glad? Everyone wants to feel pleased and delighted, right? Yes, and when you make others glad, you receive gladness in return. When you make someone smile, no doubt you are smiling yourself and that kind gesture will return to you numerous times throughout the day. Trust me. It's true.

As the angel told the shepherds who were watching their sheep that night so long ago:

> ..."*Do not be afraid, for behold, **I bring you good tidings of great joy which will be to all people**"* (Luke 2:10 NKJV).

The shepherds were chosen that night to hear the angel's proclamation of good tidings, to receive the good news of how the Savior, Christ the Lord, was born in a manger and how He would bring great joy for all people. It's all about Jesus. It should always be about Jesus.

Would the angel have to tell us not to be afraid? Would we be startled by the appearance of an angel bringing good tidings of great joy? The Lord brings us good news every day and we are not startled or even surprised; unfortunately, we seem to ignore the goodness He showers us with. Do we thank Him for the good food, weather, and job we have? Do we praise Him for the good air we breathe, family, and friends?

Not only should we share good tidings with others, we should also acknowledge the good news we live every day. We have so much to be thankful for—and when we share that goodness with others, we will shine a brighter light on what Christianity is all about.

A portion of the Gospel of Matthew is titled The Final Judgment. Jesus makes it very clear what our assignment is regarding poor, distressed, and impoverished people. He told His disciples—and us:

> But when the Son of Man comes in his glory, and all the angels with him, then he will sit upon his glorious throne. All the nations will be gathered in his presence, and he will separate the people as a shepherd separates the sheep from the goats. He will place the sheep at his right hand and the goats at his left.
>
> Then the King will say to those on his right, "Come, you who are blessed by my Father, inherit the Kingdom prepared for you from the creation of the world. For I was hungry, and you fed me. I was thirsty, and you gave me a drink. I was a stranger, and you invited me into your home. I was naked,

and you gave me clothing. I was sick, and you cared for me. I was in prison, and you visited me."

Then these righteous ones will reply, "Lord, when did we ever see you hungry and feed you? Or thirsty and give you something to drink? Or a stranger and show you hospitality? Or naked and give you clothing? When did we ever see you sick or in prison and visit you?"

*And the King will say, "I tell you the truth, **when you did it to one of the least of these my brothers and sisters, you were doing it to me!"***

Then the King will turn to those on the left and say, "Away with you, you cursed ones, into the eternal fire prepared for the devil and his demons. For I was hungry, and you didn't feed me. I was thirsty, and you didn't give me a drink. I was a stranger, and you didn't invite me into your home. I was naked, and you didn't give me clothing. I was sick and in prison, and you didn't visit me."

Then they will reply, "Lord, when did we ever see you hungry or thirsty or a stranger or naked or sick or in prison, and not help you?"

*And he will answer, "I tell you the truth, **when you refused to help the least of these my brothers and sisters, you were refusing to help me."***

And they will go away into eternal punishment, but the righteous will go into eternal life (Matthew 25:31-46).

This admonition from Jesus is a bit daunting—and a lot exciting. Spending eternal life with God the Father in a mansion He built just for us is wonderful beyond our imagination. We can rest assured that our names are written in Heaven's "reservation" book—that we will enjoy the presence of the Lord as we praise and worship Him in Heaven.

The daunting part of the Scripture passage, of course, is feeling a bit convicted of the times when we could have:

- fed the hungry guy on the corner holding the sign
- offered a hot and tired jogger a bottle of water
- invited a stranger to church for a meal

- donated clothes and shoes to the Salvation Army

- volunteered at the local elderly care home or Hospice

- visited a person in prison—be it an emotional, mental, spiritual, or physical prison

Jesus says when we do these types of selfless acts of kindness and goodness, we are doing them to Him. We are demonstrating the good tidings that were brought to earth that starry night so many years ago in the little town of Bethlehem.

Ruach City Church has a program called Koinonia. This is where people within the church or in the community can receive free food and free non-perishable items (diapers, soap powder, etc.). We sometimes even pay people's electricity and gas and provide travel expenses, if they have a job interview and are struggling at that particular time in their lives. We also support them spiritually and pray that the Lord will change their situation. We've received countless testimonies of people's lives and circumstances changing. A simple act of giving and love can make all the difference!

We feed the homeless every week with hot meals and provide them clothes of good quality. We do not take soiled clothes or damaged items. We also provide them with information about where they can get assistance for various issues they are facing. It is one of our missions to provide shelter and on-going help for people who are less unfortunate.

Jesus never lost sight of His assignment—we shouldn't either. Throughout the ages there were people who saw a need in another and met it. Excellent examples:

THE GOOD SAMARITAN

Jesus replied with a story: "A Jewish man was traveling from Jerusalem down to Jericho, and he was attacked by bandits. They stripped him of his clothes, beat him up, and left him half dead beside the road. By chance a priest came along. But when he saw the man lying there, he crossed to the other side of the road and passed him by. A Temple assistant walked over and looked at him lying there, but he also passed by on the other side. Then a despised Samaritan came along, and when he saw the man, he felt compassion for him. Going over to him, the Samaritan soothed his wounds with olive oil and wine and bandaged them. Then he put the man on his own donkey and took him to an inn, where he took care of him. The next day he handed the innkeeper two silver coins, telling him, "Take care of this man. If his bill runs higher than this, I'll pay you the next time I'm here." Now which of these three would you say was a neighbor to the man who was attacked by bandits?" Jesus asked. The man replied, "The one who showed him mercy." Then Jesus said, "Yes, now go and do the same" (Luke 10:30-38).

WILLIAM AND CATHERINE BOOTH

In 1865, William Booth was invited to hold a series of evangelistic meetings in the East End of London. He set up a tent in a Quaker graveyard, and his services became an instant success. This proved to be the end of his wanderings as an independent traveling evangelist. His renown as a religious leader spread throughout London, and he attracted followers who were dedicated to fight for the souls of men and women.

Thieves, prostitutes, gamblers, and drunkards were among Booth's first converts to Christianity. To congregations who were desperately poor, he preached hope and salvation. His aim was to lead people to Christ and link them to a church for further spiritual guidance.

Many churches, however, did not accept Booth's followers because of their past. So Booth continued giving his new converts spiritual direction, challenging them to save others like themselves. Soon, they too were preaching and singing in the streets as a living testimony to the power of God.[1]

The Salvation Army's ministries include: prison ministries, elderly services, hunger relief, housing and homeless services, adult rehabilitation, emergency disaster services, and veterans affairs services. William and Catherine Booth committed their lives to preaching and reaching the poor, distressed, and impoverished; their commitment has spread worldwide. In the United States in the year

2015, approximately 30 million people received meaningful help from the Salvation Army.[2]

MOTHER TERESA

A Catholic nun, Mother Teresa taught in India for 17 years before she experienced her 1946 "call within a call" to devote herself to caring for the sick and poor. Her order established a hospice; centers for the blind, aged, and disabled; and a leper colony. In 1979 she received the Nobel Peace Prize for her humanitarian work.

A portion of the Nobel Prize organization's biography of Mother Teresa follows:

> In 1948 Mother Teresa received permission from her superiors to leave the convent school and devote herself to working among the poorest of the poor in the slums of Calcutta. Although she had no funds, she depended on Divine Providence, and started an open-air school for slum children. Soon she was joined by voluntary helpers, and financial support was also forthcoming. This made it possible for her to extend the scope of her work.
>
> On October 7, 1950, Mother Teresa received permission from the Holy See to start her own order, "The Missionaries of Charity," whose primary task was to love and care for those persons nobody was prepared to look after. In 1965 the Society became an International Religious Family by a decree of Pope Paul VI.
>
> The Society of Missionaries has spread all over the world, including the former Soviet Union and Eastern European countries. They provide effective help to the poorest of the poor in a number of countries in Asia, Africa, and Latin America, and they undertake relief work in the wake of natural catastrophes such as floods, epidemics, and famine, and for refugees. The order also has houses in North America, Europe and Australia, where they take care of the shut-ins, alcoholics, homeless, and AIDS sufferers.

The Missionaries of Charity throughout the world are aided and assisted by Co-Workers who became an official International Association on March 29, 1969. By the 1990s there were over one million Co-Workers in more than 40 countries. Along with the Co-Workers, the lay Missionaries of Charity try to follow Mother Teresa's spirit and charism in their families.[3]

These are only a few of the people who worked tirelessly fulfilling their God-given assignments—those written about in Isaiah 61 and spoken about by Jesus in Luke 4. Many people only known to those they help are sitting beside you in church, on the subway and the bus, in the classroom and the boardroom.

Are you ready to take your assignment seriously?

ENDNOTES

1. http://www.salvationarmyusa.org/usn/history-of-the-salvation-army; accessed January 22, 2016.

2. http://www.salvationarmyusa.org/usn/ways-we-help; accessed January 22, 2016.

3. http://www.nobelprize.org/nobel_prizes/peace/laureates/1979/teresa-bio.html; accessed January 22, 2016.

Chapter 6

HEALING THE
BROKENHEARTED

*The Spirit of the Lord is upon Me, because He has anointed Me to preach the gospel to the poor; He has sent Me to **heal the brokenhearted**...*
(Luke 4:18 NKJV).

W e are to heal broken and damaged people—and there are a lot of them. Maybe you were one—or are one now. When you seek to heal others, you will be healed as well. Jesus healed the brokenhearted when He walked the earth. Now, we are the ones He assigned to help and heal those with whom we walk alongside in life.

People hurt people and we need to be available to restore the trust they lost. People let people down and do rotten things to each other. We must show them that followers of Christ are different—we can be trusted, we can love, we can heal. We have been empowered to help people. How? By our words and our deeds.

The church is supposed to be a place of healing—a hospital where sick people come to be helped and healed. Everyone who walks through the doors of a church enter as people who are sick. We all have a sickness of some kind, and Jesus came so that all can be healed. Now He expects us to use our anointing to heal the sick.

Jesus said that healthy people don't need a doctor—sick people do.

When Jesus heard this, he told them, "Healthy people don't need a doctor— sick people do. I have come to call not those who think they are righteous, but those who know they are sinners" (Mark 2:17).

The church is a place of healing. We need to bring people to church so they can be healed. No one wants to be sick, no one wants to suffer, no one wants to lay around feeling as if life has no meaning. No. We must lead them to the One who can heal every sickness, relieve every suffering heart and spirit, lift up every sad soul with hope and the thrill of living an exciting life of wholeness and joy!

I strongly believe that this year is the year of the Lord's favor and as such, during this year and subsequent years, the church will begin to be filled with sick and hurting people coming in search of healing. Churches need to get ready to receive these broken and damaged people. We need to realize that the Lord is driving them toward the church—so we can welcome them in His name and for His glory.

Let's make our churches places where people can come to be healed. Let's make our churches houses of favor—kindness. Let's make our churches Bethesda pools of healing.

Afterward Jesus returned to Jerusalem for one of the Jewish holy days. Inside the city, near the Sheep Gate, was the pool of Bethesda [house of favor], with five covered porches. Crowds of sick people—blind, lame, or paralyzed—lay on the porches. One of the men lying there had been sick for thirty-eight years. When Jesus saw him and knew he had been ill for a long time, he asked him, "Would you like to get well?" "I can't, sir," the sick man said, "for I have no one to put me into the pool when the water bubbles up. Someone else always gets there ahead of me." Jesus told him, "Stand up, pick up your mat, and walk!" Instantly, the man was healed! He rolled up his sleeping mat and began walking!... (John 5:1-9).

I like the King James Version better: "[Jesus] saith unto him, Wilt thou be made whole?" Jesus knew this man needed to be made whole—physiologically, mentally, and physically. He knew this guy was so messed up that he couldn't get himself together. Jesus was anointed to heal broken and damaged people—the brokenhearted, mentally downtrodden, the spiritually dead.

Jesus knew the man didn't have to wait for the pool to bubble to be healed. Jesus knew that the man didn't have to have his heart broken again from seeing others healed while he remained sick. Jesus knew that He was empowered to heal the man wholly, completely through the anointing, through the grace of God on His life.

We can know the same—we know the Great Physician and He reigns and rules and heals in our churches and our homes and our spirits. Believers have the assurance of God's healing power and all we have to do is ask, seek, and knock on His office door.

> *Ask, and it will be given to you; **seek**, and you will find; **knock**, and it will be opened to you. For everyone who asks receives, and he who seeks finds, and to him who knocks it will be opened. Or what man is there among you who, if his son asks for bread, will give him a stone? Or if he asks for a fish, will he give him a serpent? If you then, being evil, know how to give good gifts to your children, **how much more will your Father who is in heaven give good things to those who ask Him!** (Matthew 7:7-11 NKJV)

The Great Physician's office hours are 24-7, 365 days a year—no exceptions. I pray and prophesy that churches worldwide will become sanctuaries of healing, of wholeness. As we open wide the church doors and the brokenhearted enter in, they will feel the peace that passes their understanding, they will absorb the Lord's mercy, they will accept Jesus as their Savior. Healing will completely envelope them and they will never be the same again.

We have the power to change people's lives—if we connect with them, if we reach out to them, if we love them.

In an interesting story about physical healing and also heart healing, I was amazed and encouraged by the following modern-day miracle that a young girl experienced and spoke about on television in April 2015:

> Annabel Beam was just five years old when she was diagnosed with two incurable disorders. Treatments for pseudo-obstruction motility disorder and antral hypomotility disorder—life-threatening digestive disorders—kept her in and out of the hospital for years.

In 2011, another tragedy struck. While Annabel was climbing a tree, a branch gave way, sending Annabel falling 30 feet head-first into a hollowed-out cottonwood tree. After several hours, an emergency fire crew managed to harness Annabel to safety and she was rushed to the hospital in a helicopter. Incredibly, not only did Annabel survive the terrible fall without injury, the symptoms of her disorders miraculously disappeared.

Annabel's mother, Christy,...explained that her daughter was in constant pain for much of her childhood. At one point Annabel even said that she wanted to die and go to heaven to live with Jesus.

Annabel revealed that when she fell out of the tree and was unconscious, she actually visited heaven, "I saw heaven and it was really bright, and I saw my Mimi who had died a couple years back," Annabel explained. "And that's how I knew I was in heaven. I believe that I was cured because...I asked Jesus if I could stay with him, and he said, 'No, Annabel, I have plans for you on Earth that you cannot fulfill in heaven.... Whenever I send you back, there will be nothing wrong with you,'" Annabel said.

Since the accident, Annabel has not been hospitalized for her digestive disorders, which has confounded doctors. Christy revealed that Annabel is now asymptomatic and is currently on zero medications.[1]

You may have read or witnessed other miracles of healing. Each is proof of God's sincere desire for us to be whole. He is waiting for us to ask Him to make us whole, to make us well, to heal our sickness.

There was a time in one of our services when someone was diagnosed with cancer and I felt led to throw my hanky on him—the cloth that I use to wipe my face when I'm preaching. As I threw it on the person, he fell down by the power of the Holy Spirit and he said he felt that he had been healed from within. A report from the doctor later that week confirmed that he had been healed of cancer—he was cancer free. Needless to say I didn't get my hanky back. I strongly believe that there is power in whatever we wear or use when it's serving God's purpose and to show His glory. The Bible tells us in Acts 19:12 (NIV): *"that even handkerchiefs and aprons that had touched him* [Paul] *were taken to the sick, and their illnesses were cured and the evil spirits left them."*

And I will never forget this story. I was preaching in the United States at a conference called Praise Power. A lady came forward in a wheelchair who also had been diagnosed with cancer. She was in a bad way, but I felt led to wrap her in my prayer shawl. Then I saw angels all around her. I told her that she should get up and start to walk and that her faith will make her whole. She believed the word and started to rise up from the wheelchair and started to walk, declaring that she had been healed. All who saw her noticed the difference in her countenance immediately. The following year, I was invited back to preach at the same conference and the lady came back to testify and show everyone her doctor's report revealing how she was completely healed of cancer. Other healings and miracles took place that night also, it was amazing. People started to run over to the corner where I said I saw angels and were jumping and shouting, claiming their healing too.

But how about the healings that take place within, the hurts that are so deep that our hearts actually hurt. I'm sure you have read or heard of couples who were married for a long time and when one spouse passes away the other passes not long after. I believe people can die from broken hearts. We can become so distressed that we give up on life. That is sad, tragic really, because as it seems Jesus told Annabel, her assignment on earth needed to be completed before she spent eternity with Him in Heaven.

If you feel as if life isn't worth living, always remember that Psalm 34:18 says, *"The Lord is close to the brokenhearted; he rescues those whose spirits are crushed."* Have you ever felt crushed, broken, deeply in despair? There is hope and healing available to you in the blink of an eye. First you have to acknowledge your situation, then you have to reach out to God, asking Him to restore you, to make you whole again.

Only when you are whole and healed can you help others.

Only when we are whole and healed can we help others. As said many times by many people and even posted on bumper stickers, "Christians aren't perfect, just forgiven" and "A Christian is a work in progress." Both sayings are true, and we must realize that there was only one perfect Man—Jesus. While on earth we should be constantly trying to mature in our faith; renewing our minds as God gives us revelations and insights.

We receive His wisdom every time we read His Word—the Bible. His Love Letter to us is filled with advice and solutions to fit every situation we will ever face in life. If you sincerely believe Jesus is your Wonderful Counselor, Mighty God, Everlasting Father, and Prince of Peace,[2] then you will want to know as much as possible about Him. Reading and meditating on Scripture, allowing the Holy Spirit to bring you revelation will bring you closer to Him. Also, pastors who are anointed and filled with the Holy Spirit can teach us things about our heavenly Father that we may never know otherwise. God holds church and ministry leaders to a higher standard; therefore, we will most probably be able to discern who is telling us the truth of His Word. Nevertheless, we must be careful, vigilant about who we allow into our lives. It is written in 2 Peter 2:1-3:

> But **there were also false prophets in Israel, just as there will be false teachers among you.** *They will cleverly teach destructive heresies and even deny the Master who bought them. In this way, they will bring sudden destruction on themselves. Many will follow their evil teaching and shameful immorality. And because of these teachers, the way of truth will be slandered. In their greed they will make up clever lies to get hold of your money. But God condemned them long ago, and their destruction will not be delayed.*

We must be wise as owls—watching for signs of true prophets, for the fruit of their words and actions. Please read the entire second chapter of 2 Peter as the writer is very specific about who to trust and who to stay away from. I suggest you read this chapter in several different Bible translations as each has insights that may be more clear than others—so you can fully understand the seriousness of the warnings. The chapter discusses topics that are in the news today and that cause dissention among church leadership and church family members. The Bible makes clear God's stand on these matters—and you must take a stand according to what God reveals to you.

In addition to 2 Peter, Acts, Galatians, and 1 Timothy also mention false teachers and provide insight into how important it is to beware:

I know that false teachers, like vicious wolves, will come in among you after I leave, not sparing the flock (Acts 20:29).

Those false teachers are so eager to win your favor, but their intentions are not good. They are trying to shut you off from me so that you will pay attention only to them (Galatians 4:17).

Now the Holy Spirit tells us clearly that in the last times some will turn away from the true faith; they will follow deceptive spirits and teachings that come from demons (1 Timothy 4:1).

These are serious facts of life that believers must take to heart—lest we become brokenhearted. Many have been deceived already and are in need of healing. Many have put their faith in people who let them down, betrayed their trust, or turned out to be a wolf in sheep's clothing. How about our clothing? How are we to dress as Christians? Ephesians 6:10-17 says:

*A final word: Be strong in the Lord and in his mighty power. **Put on all of God's armor so that you will be able to stand firm against all strategies of the devil.** For we are not fighting against flesh-and-blood enemies, but against evil rulers and authorities of the unseen world, against mighty powers in this dark world, and against evil spirits in the heavenly places. Therefore, put on every piece of God's armor so you will be able to resist the enemy in the time of evil. Then after the battle you will still be standing firm. Stand your ground, putting on the **belt of truth** and the **body armor** of God's righteousness. For **shoes, put on the peace** that comes from the Good News so that you will be fully prepared. In addition to all of these, hold up the **shield of faith** to stop the fiery arrows of the devil. Put on **salvation as your helmet**, and take the **sword of the Spirit**, which is the word of God* [Bible].

These articles of clothing are for waging and winning wars! But on the other hand, Colossians 3:12 says:

*Since God chose you to be the holy people he loves, **you must clothe yourselves with tenderhearted mercy, kindness, humility, gentleness, and patience.***

Do these two passages of Scripture seem to be contradictory? Well, they really aren't. When you delve into God's Word—really delve deeply with the help of the Holy Spirit, you will quickly realize that He gives you the truth you need at the specific time you need it. For example, when dealing with different personalities or attitudes or attacks, you may need to strap on the body armor of God's righteousness to deflect harmful spirit-piercing arrows of deceit. Or maybe you are trying to connect with a co-worker who you know for a fact is seeking Christ's forgiveness; then you must clothe yourself with tenderhearted mercy, kindness, humility, gentleness, and patience.

God's Word, enlightened into your mind and spirit by the Holy Spirit, will never let you down, never leave you speechless, and never abandon you in times of trouble, confrontation, or when reaching out in faith to the brokenhearted with a healing touch.

As we pass by people of all shapes and color and backgrounds every day on the way to work or the grocery store, may we remember that what is going on in their minds or behind their front doors could be tragic. People don't always wear their brokenheartedness for all to see. Many hide it away, keep it bottled up inside where the hurt festers and causes all types of problems, including physical ailments.

The following is a report from the American Heart Association worth noting about broken hearts:

> When you think of a broken heart, you may picture a cartoon drawing with a jagged line through it. But a real-life broken heart can actually lead to cardiac consequences. There are established ties between depression, mental health and heart disease. Read on for more information about how an extremely stressful event can have an impact on your heart.

BREAKDOWN OF A BROKEN HEART

> Broken heart syndrome, also called stress-induced cardiomyopathy or takotsubo cardiomyopathy, can strike even if you're healthy. (Tako tsubo, by the way, are octopus traps that resemble the pot-like shape of the stricken heart.)

Women are more likely than men to experience the sudden, intense chest pain—the reaction to a surge of stress hormones—that can be caused by an emotionally stressful event. It could be the death of a loved one or even a divorce, breakup or physical separation, betrayal or romantic rejection. It could even happen after a good shock (like winning the lottery.)

Broken heart syndrome may be misdiagnosed as a heart attack because the symptoms and test results are similar. In fact, tests show dramatic changes in rhythm and blood substances that are typical of a heart attack. But unlike a heart attack, there's no evidence of blocked heart arteries in broken heart syndrome.

In broken heart syndrome, a part of your heart temporarily enlarges and doesn't pump well, while the rest of your heart functions normally or with even more forceful contractions. Researchers are just starting to learn the causes, and how to diagnose and treat it.

The bad news: Broken heart syndrome can lead to severe, short-term heart muscle failure.

The good news: Broken heart syndrome is usually treatable. Most people who experience it make a full recovery within weeks, and they're at low risk for it happening again (although in rare cases in can be fatal).

What to Look for: Signs and Symptoms The most common signs and symptoms of broken heart syndrome are angina (chest pain) and shortness of breath. You can experience these things even if you have no history of heart disease.

Arrhythmias (irregular heartbeats) or cardiogenic shock also may occur with broken heart syndrome. Cardiogenic shock is a condition in which a suddenly weakened heart can't pump enough blood to meet the body's needs, and it can be fatal if it isn't treated right away. (When people die from heart attacks, cardiogenic shock is the most common cause of death.)[3]

I encourage you to take a moment or two to speak kindly to the person beside you in line at the bank or the coffee shop. To offer your seat to someone on the bus or give up your favorite seat in church to someone searching for a place to sit. To smile at everyone you meet along the way every day. Clothe yourself with lovingkindness and you will make a huge difference in the lives of others—and give yourself a character-building boost.

Unlike when you are standing at the closet choosing your clothes for a day at the office or the factory or for a party or a trip to the market, the Lord has already chosen the clothes that you need to wear for each and every occasion in your life. Like Adam and Eve, you will never "feel naked"[4] as God the Father has provided clothing that will never go out of style or make you feel ashamed.

Jesus's assignment and purpose was to give us a rich and satisfying life—the devil's purpose is to steal, kill, and destroy[5]—and keep people bound and bullied into a life of defeat. In the next chapter we will examine how we are to proclaim freedom for the prisoners.

ENDNOTES

1. "Miracles from Heaven": Near-Fatal Fall Cures Sick Little Girl's Symptoms; FoxNews-Insider, April 14, 2015; http://insider.foxnews.com/2015/04/14/miracles-heaven-near-fatal-fall-cures-sick-little-girls-symptoms; accessed January 22, 2016.

2. Isaiah 9:6.

3. http://www.heart.org/HEARTORG/Conditions/More/Cardiomyopathy/Is-Broken-Heart-Syndrome-Real_UCM_448547_Article.jsp#.VsSTTzHSmM8; accessed February 17, 2016.

4. See Genesis 3:7,10.

5. See John 10:10.

Chapter 7

PROCLAIMING LIBERTY

The Spirit of the Lord is upon Me, because He has anointed Me to preach the gospel to the poor; He has sent Me to heal the brokenhearted, to pro-claim liberty to the captives and recovery of sight to the blind, to set at liberty those who are oppressed... (Luke 4:18-19 NKJV).

Captivity is a form of slavery, it's bondage. People in captivity are brainwashed and become the property of the one who controls their freedom. When God's people were taken into Babylonian captivity, the Babylonians changed everything about God's people's existence to ensure that they could keep them under control. They changed their names (identity). They changed their language (history). They changed their food (tradition). They changed their religion (spiritual identity).

Captors mess with their captives' minds. They fill their minds with falsehoods, perverted reality. Those reading this book are most probably not captives in the way the Israelites were captives in Babylon. But many reading this book are captives of the devil and his minions who seek to terrorize and destroy.

Being held captive is not only a physical restriction but also a situation that plays on a person's mind. There are countless modern-day true stories about how the treatment of prisoners of war focuses on the mind as much as it inflicts torture on the body.

To prevent the devil from invading our minds, we must consistently occupy our minds with godly, righteous thoughts. If we neglect to fill the void in our minds, selfish and devilish thoughts will invade and set up camp. Wherever there is a void it must be filled with something. That's why the Israelites were told in the Old Testament to occupy their minds:

> This **Book of the Law** shall not depart from your mouth, but you shall **read [and meditate on] it day and night**, so that you may be careful to do [everything] in accordance with all that is written in it; for then you will make **your way prosperous, and then you will be successful** (Joshua 1:8 AMP).

And why the New Testament tells us:

> Finally, believers, whatever is **true**, whatever is **honorable and worthy of respect**, whatever is **right and confirmed by God's word**, whatever is **pure and wholesome**, whatever is **lovely and brings peace**, whatever is **admirable and of good repute**; if there is any **excellence**, if there is anything **worthy of praise, think continually on these things [center your mind on them, and implant them in your heart]** (Philippians 4:8 AMP).

We must realize the importance of keeping our minds focused on God's Word. When we have open minds, we are open for any foolishness. This reminds me of a true story of a time in the West Indies when I was in a church service and the leader said that he would leave the service open for someone to come up and say something. Well, there was a woman there we called Mother Shaw, and when she heard that the service was to be left open, she said, "I don't like to let anything open...cause then anything can come and fly right in it." She was right!

If we don't have our minds filled to overflowing with Scripture and praise and worship and good thoughts for others, anyone can come to us and say anything and we will believe it. This should not be so! When someone comes and prophesies over you and you know it contradicts God's Word, you can tell the person, "Thank you for the prophecy but I do not receive it because I know what God told me and I know what I have inside of me. If you lay hands on me and prophesy, you should only be confirming what I already know."

Prophecies should confirm what you already know to be true according to God's Word.

If you find yourself being held captive by the past or an uncertain future or family curses or addiction, or whatever—no matter how much of yourself is affected by captivity, God can fully restore you—and more! Take, for example, when Job was being held captive by the devil and his family and fortune and health was taken away from him. Job 42:10 says:

*When Job prayed for his friends, **the Lord restored** his fortunes. In fact, the Lord gave him **twice as much** as before!*

You can break every chain and every tie that is binding you—by using God's Word as your weapon. John 1:1 says: *"In the beginning the Word already existed. The Word was with God, and the Word was God."* Jesus is the Word and He should be your weapon of choice when seeking a breakthrough. When the devil tempted Jesus in the wilderness for 40 days, what was Jesus's weapon? *"The Scriptures say...,"* *The Scriptures also say..."* and *"For the Scriptures say..."* (Matthew 4:4,7,10).

If Jesus used God's Word, the Scriptures, as His sure victory over the devil, how much more should we rely on the wisdom contained in His Love Letter to us! Jesus was tempted 40 days and nights while on earth. At times it may feel as if we are being tested 365 days a year. The more battered and bruised we feel, the more we need to open the Word and sink ourselves into it as deeply as possible.

I know from much personal experience that you will emerge from your time in the Word with a joyful outlook and an energetic excitement for whatever challenge may come your way. You will take on that uncooperative co-worker with ease, you will give that rebellious teenager the loving hug he needs, you will welcome the difficult talk you know you need to have with that sister in the Lord who is traveling down the wrong path.

Part of our assignment is to proclaim liberty to the captives (Isaiah 61:1), to announce freedom, liberty. John 8:36 (NKJV) says, *"Therefore if the Son makes you free, you shall be free indeed."* And Galatians 5:1 (NKJV) says, *"Stand fast therefore in the liberty by which Christ has made us free, and do not be entangled again with a yoke of bondage."* The message of Jesus Christ is one of freedom and liberty. How we conduct ourselves as we go about our assignment should reflect this truth.

If we walk around as if under a grey cloud of negativity and talk as if gloom and doom is hovering over us, people will immediately notice that attitude and mindset and will want nothing to do with us or with Christianity.

A merry heart makes a cheerful countenance, but by sorrow of the heart the spirit is broken (Proverbs 15:13 NKJV).

And James 5:13 says: *"Are any of you suffering hardships? You should pray. Are any of you happy? You should sing praises."* We Christians, born-again believers, followers of Christ have much to be happy about! Therefore, we need to sing and shout and proclaim liberty as loudly as possible every chance we get to do so. When our countenance, our outward expression, is one of joy with smiles and sparkling eyes, people will be immediately drawn to us—they will want what we have.

Sometimes a smile and a pat on the back or a gentle hug is all someone needs to melt his or her heart enough to listen to your story of salvation. Sometimes a sincere act of kindness is all that people need to embrace the story of Jesus, the Savior.

A recent story that caught my attention on social media happened in Ireland and the story has "gone viral":

> As an elderly woman was getting off the bus, she almost tripped. Once she was off, the bus driver noticed that her shoe lace was undone and he stalled the bus to tell her. When she said that she knew, he realized that she wasn't steady enough on her feet to bend down and tie it herself, so he got off the bus and tied it for her. A passenger on the bus commented, "I haven't seen someone do something so kind in as long as I can remember and the lady was so appreciative she blew a kiss as the bus was pulling away."

Not only did the man's selfless act of kindness affect the elderly woman but also passengers on the bus and most likely more people who were passing by on the street. Such a seemingly small act had a huge impact on countless people worldwide. That is the type of impact God is assigning to us.

Take the time to be kind to someone.

Take a few minutes to think about what you can do to make a difference in someone's life today. Be it small and seemingly insignificant, just do it. God can multiply the effect hundreds, thousands, even millions of times. When you take the time to be kind to someone, not only will you make them smile, you will smile as well. "What goes around comes around," they say. God's Word says, *"Do to others as you would like them to do to you"* (Luke 6:31).

I recall one time when I was in the United States, shopping with my daughters, I heard a lady crying in the shopping mall and screaming at her son. Apparently she gave him some bags to carry and he forgot to pick up one of the bags by accident—the one with her purse in it. She was frantic and ready to beat him publicly. I approached her and asked what happened and she told us. She was brokenhearted because she said it had all her money in there for the week; she didn't know how she would feed the children. I managed to calm her down and gave her $200 and prayed with her. She was so relieved and thanked the Lord for making our paths meet. I prayed with her right there in the shopping mall and she gave her life to the Lord.

It is also important to understand that our acts of kindness need not bring us attention. We should be acting out of obedience to the Lord, out of the goodness of our hearts. We need no thank you, no reward, no glory. All the glory must go to our heavenly Father who has softened our hard hearts to want to generously give, to want to help others come to know the ultimate kindness of God who sent His Son to proclaim victory over death.

When we proclaim victory, we are proclaiming liberty from being self-absorbed, being addicted, living according to the flesh, which leads to death. When we shout victory that the captives are being released, we are proclaiming God's ultimate conquest over death and dying. When we show compassion to others, we are in reality proclaiming hope to all and opening the door to introduce them to Jesus, *"the way, the truth, and the life"* (John 14:6).

OPENING PERSONAL PRISONS

Our assignment ensures that those who are bound will be given a way out. Our assignment is to help others break out of whatever has become a prison to them—to open their eyes and unburden those who are yoked and feel held back.

To open blinded eyes means to illuminate, brighten their outlook. When people are feeling down and out, their gaze is toward the ground, it's hazy and hampered. Our assignment is to open their eyes to the sunny skies above that are beaming with opportunities and shining with love and hope!

When people are yoked, joined together, with ungodly people or environments or substances, they lose their vision—they can't see or move on their own because they are tied tightly to something or someone other than God. Some people realize this unrighteous yoke and others have lived with it so long that they don't know what life could be like if unyoked—if set free from their personal prison. They need a breakthrough.

We are assigned to provide that breakthrough for people. Your assignment is to destroy everything that is not of God—every demon, soothsayer, every generational curse, every addiction, every fleshly desire. We need to use our anointing to change the world around us, the people we know and don't know. The devil can't stop us!

*And, behold, there was a woman which had a spirit of infirmity eighteen years, and was bowed together, and could in no wise lift up herself. And when Jesus saw her, he called her to him, and said unto her, **Woman, thou art loosed** from thine infirmity* (Luke 13:11-12 KJV).

*[Jesus] saw a woman who had been crippled by an evil spirit. She had been bent double for eighteen years and was unable to stand up straight. When Jesus saw her, he called her over and said, "Dear woman, **you are healed** of your sickness!"* (Luke 13:11-12)

T. D. Jakes pastors a very large church in Texas in the United States. He wrote a book some years ago titled, *Woman, Thou Art Loosed*. In that book he proclaimed truth about how women in particular can build self-made prisons that prevent them from becoming who God intended. A few excerpts from his book may ring true for you or for someone you know. I pray that the following will help you or others to be loosed from the yoke holding you back.

Her problem didn't begin suddenly. It had existed in her life for
18 years. We are looking at a woman who had a personal war

going on inside her. These struggles must have tainted many other areas of her life. The infirmity that attacked her life was physical. However, many women also wrestle with infirmities in emotional traumas. These infirmities can be just as challenging as a physical affliction. An emotional handicap can create dependence on many different levels. Relationships can become crutches. The infirmed woman then places such weight on people that it stresses a healthy relationship. Many times such emotional handicaps will spawn a series of unhealthy relationships.

...Healing cannot come to a desperate person rummaging through other people's lives. One of the first things that a hurting person needs to do is break the habit of using other people as a narcotic to numb the dull aching of an inner void. The more you medicate the symptoms, the less chance you have of allowing God to heal you. The other destructive tendency that can exist with any abuse is the person must keep increasing the dosage.

Avoid addictive, obsessive relationships. If you are becoming increasingly dependent upon anything other than God to create a sense of wholeness in your life, then you are abusing your relationships. Clinging to people is far different from loving them. It is not so much a statement of your love for them as it is a crying out of your need for them. Like lust, it is intensely selfish. It is taking and not giving. Love is giving. God is love. God proved His love not by His need of us, but by His giving to us.

The Scriptures plainly show that this infirmed woman had tried to lift herself. People who stand on the outside can easily criticize and assume that the infirmed woman lacks effort and fortitude. That is not always the case. Some situations in which we find ourselves defy will power. We feel unable to change.

The Scriptures say that she "could in no wise lift up herself." That implies she had employed various means of self-ministry. Isn't it amazing how the same people who lift up countless others, often cannot lift themselves? The type of person may be a tower of faith and prayer for others, but impotent when it comes to her own limitations. ...Sometimes we esteem others more important than ourselves. We always become the martyr.

It is wonderful to be self-sacrificing but watch out for self-disdain! If we don't apply some of the medicine that we use on others to strengthen ourselves, our patients will be healed and we will be dying.[1]

Bishop Jakes goes on to explain how our self-made prisons are not strong enough to withstand a powerful jolt of God's anointing. He espouses that there is deep cleansing available for those seemingly inaccessible areas of the feminine heart. Women—and men—can fight back the infections of life by leaning on the Great Physician who has a prescription for every ailment.

After trauma or tragedy, men and women alike can build sky-high walls or place themselves in locked cages to protect against being hurt or abused. The trouble with these barriers? They keep out the "good guys"! We must be the "good guys" who are willing to scale the walls and pick the cage locks. Too many of God's children are cowering in the corner of their prison cell, unwilling to venture out far enough to hear us proclaiming the good news—the trumpet sounding the victory. Therefore, our assignment is to reach into their world with the love and mercy and grace of our forgiving heavenly Father.

Physical Prisons

There are indeed those who have committed crimes and are living within a physical prison where their every move is controlled. Every moment of every day is dictated by those in authority over them. Many churches have prison outreaches and make a tremendous difference in the lives of the men and women serving their time to "pay" for their offenses. Some prisoners don't take the outreaches seriously, but others do and that is why Christians keep reaching out—as it says in the Bible we should (Matthew 25:31-46).

A compassionate and meaningful ministry established by a former prisoner, Charles Colson, has reached hundreds of thousands of children in the United States whose parents are incarcerated. From the organization's Website:

Children often feel lonely and abandoned when their mom or dad goes away to prison. But Prison Fellowship's Angel Tree program is here to help. Church volunteers around the country provide local children with the Gospel message and Christmas gifts on behalf of their incarcerated parent. These children also receive a special message from their mom or dad, reminding them of their love. Through Angel Tree, churches are coming alongside families of the incarcerated at Christmastime, and all year long, to provide support while their loved ones are away. Every child has a story. For 2.7 million American children, that story is filled with the abandonment, loneliness, and shame that come from having a mom or dad in prison. For many, it may also include following their parents down the same destructive road to incarceration.

Angel Tree, a program of Prison Fellowship, reaches out to the children of inmates and their families with the love of Christ. This unique program gives your church an opportunity to share Christ's love by helping to meet the physical, emotional, and spiritual needs of the families of prisoners.

Prison Fellowship seeks to restore those affected by crime and incarceration by introducing prisoners, victims, and their families to a new hope available through Jesus Christ. By nurturing a growing Christian community inside America's prisons, as well as equipping churches and communities to welcome those men and women home once they finish their sentences, restoration and healing can begin. To accomplish this, we train and inspire churches and communities—inside and outside of prison—to support the restoration of those affected by incarceration.

330,000 plus children connected to a church in 2014 to receive the Gospel and a Christmas gift on behalf of an incarcerated parent.[2]

This is only one example of thousands of Christian ministries worldwide that take seriously the anointed assignment given to believers by God. No doubt you know of people and churches and ministries and missionaries who daily walk in their assignments with power from on high.

Let us be the ones who are willing to stand up and walk forward in our assignments so His Kingdom will come on earth as it is in Heaven (see Matthew 6:9-13).

ENDNOTES

1. Bishop T.D. Jakes, *Woman, Thou Art Loosed!* (Shippensburg, PA: Treasure House, 1993), 14-16.

2. https://www.prisonfellowship.org/resources/angel-tree/; accessed January 23, 2016.

Chapter 8

PROCLAIMING THE ACCEPTABLE YEAR OF THE LORD

The Spirit of the Lord is upon Me, because He has anointed Me to preach the gospel to the poor; He has sent Me to heal the brokenhearted, to proclaim liberty to the captives and recovery of sight to the blind, to set at liberty those who are oppressed; to **proclaim the acceptable year of the Lord.** *Then He [Jesus] closed the book, and gave it back to the attendant and sat down. And the eyes of all who were in the synagogue were fixed on Him* (Luke 4:18-20 NKJV).

Jesus read only a portion of Isaiah 61. He stopped after reading, *"to proclaim the acceptable year of the Lord."* He was confirming who He was and what His assignment was—the one given to Him by His heavenly Father. The One the prophet spoke about centuries prior to His actual physical arrival on earth.

Some Bible commentators state that the acceptable year of the Lord is alluding to the year of jubilee, when all, both debtors and servants, were set free. When Jesus read the Scripture in Isaiah 61, He proclaimed the acceptable year of the Lord, telling the world that He was the One who came from Heaven and would preach the Gospel to the poor, heal the brokenhearted, liberate the captives and the oppressed, bring sight to the blind, and usher in a new era—one based on love and grace and mercy rather than the law.

Our assignment is to announce, proclaim, shout—make known by naming the year, The Lord's Favor. What is favor? Favor is a special preference or privilege that gives someone or something an advantage over others. It is the kindness of God to favor His children.

I borrow wisdom from Pastor Billy Graham's son, Franklin, to make the point:

> In the midst of a world that seems increasingly dark and difficult, the Bible tells us that, from God's perspective, we are living in an extremely favorable time.
>
> When Jesus was handed the scroll of the Prophet Isaiah at the synagogue in Nazareth, He spoke these startling words: "'The Spirit of the Lord is on me, because he has anointed me to preach good news to the poor. He has sent me to proclaim freedom for the prisoners and recovery of sight for the blind, to release the oppressed, to proclaim the year of the Lord's favor.' Then he rolled up the scroll, gave it back to the attendant and sat down. The eyes of everyone in the synagogue were fastened on him, and he began by saying to them, *'Today this scripture is fulfilled in your hearing'*" (Luke 4:17-21).
>
> Isaiah 61 goes on to proclaim not only the year of the Lord's favor but also the day of vengeance of our God. A day of judgment is coming when Christ returns. Those who have rejected Christ will face an eternity apart from the presence of God. The Bible calls this "hell."
>
> Until then, though, we are living in the year of the Lord's favor because Christ died and rose again for our sins. Salvation by grace through faith is now available to everyone who repents and believes in His atoning work on the cross.
>
> Even as bad news swirls all around us, the Good News of His forgiveness and reconciliation is freely extended.[1]

I proclaim that this is the year that the Lord is going to show favor on all those who ask of Him. He is willing and able to provide for all our needs. When we ask Him, He will favor us with whatever is in His will for us to have. We are not to ask selfishly for ourselves, but He will honor and grant our sincere and selfless requests.

People instinctively seek favor. From babies to the elderly, we want others' favor, we want others to like us and see us as special. Children want to be the favorite of their parents. They want to be the teacher's pet. When they become older, they look for favor from their peers and even join dangerous gangs if favor isn't found at home. Young adults seek favor from their co-workers and their boss. Couples yearn for favor from each other. Tragically, rather than finding favor, many people find fault. Fault with others and with themselves.

Thankfully, favor is freely given by the Lord to those who seek Him and obey His commandments. But favor is not without sacrifice. Although we can never make amends for our sins with works, we can please God and gain His favor by seeking first His Kingdom, obeying Him, and sacrificing our selfish desires for His holiness.

The Gospel of John is full of assurances that God the Father will do and give whatever we ask for in the name of Jesus:

> *And whatever you **ask in My name**, that I will do, that the Father may be glorified in the Son* (John 14:13 NKJV).

> *If you **ask** anything **in My name**, I will do it* (John 14:14 NKJV).

> *You did not choose Me, but I chose you and appointed you that you should go and bear fruit, and that your fruit should remain, that whatever you **ask the Father in My name** He may give you* (John 15:16 NKJV).

> *And in that day you will **ask** Me nothing. Most assuredly, I say to you, whatever you ask the Father **in My name** He will give you* (John 16:23 NKJV).

> *Until now you have asked nothing **in My name**. **Ask**, and you will receive, that your joy may be full* (John 16:24 NKJV).

*In that day you will **ask in My name**, and I do not say to you that I shall pray the Father for you; for the Father Himself loves you, because you have loved Me, and have believed that I came forth from God* (John 16:26-27 NKJV).

The key words in all these Scripture passages are *"in My name"* and *"ask."* The name of Jesus is above all names[2] and the name that pleases the ears of God when He hears us invoking His beloved Son's name. The name of Jesus opens the heavens and allows blessings galore to shower down upon us. What an eternal comfort to know that Jesus is right now sitting at the right hand of God the Father and making intercession for us!

*He who did not spare His own Son, but delivered Him up for us all, how shall He not with Him also freely give us all things? Who shall bring a charge against God's elect? It is God who justifies. Who is he who condemns? It is **Christ** who died, and furthermore is also risen, **who is even at the right hand of God, who also makes intercession for us*** (Romans 8:32-34 NKJV).

After we realize the importance of the name of Jesus, knowing Him as our personal Savior and Redeemer, then we have the right to ask God to provide for our needs and to grant our petitions on our behalf and on the behalf of others we lift up in intercession. God is so attune with our frailness that He provided the Holy Spirit to pray when we don't even know how to pray for others—or ourselves.

And the Holy Spirit helps us in our weakness. For example, we don't know what God wants us to pray for. But the Holy Spirit prays for us with groanings that cannot be expressed in words (Romans 8:26).

When you don't know how to help someone in pain or suffering, prayer is always the best medicine. If possible, pray immediately with the person—whether in person or over the phone or even in a text message. Don't worry about saying or writing the right words, the Holy Spirit will give you the words that the person needs to hear or read. If you hear about the need via a prayer chain or from another person and you are busy at the moment, write the request down and pray about it before you go to bed that night.

*While Jesus was here on earth, he offered prayers and pleadings, with a loud cry and tears, to the one who could rescue him from death. And **God heard his prayers** because of his deep reverence for God* (Hebrews 5:7).

Believe that prayers are heard and answered. Jesus did—we should too!

ISAIAH 61 CONTINUED

The New Living Translation of Isaiah 61 that continues from the point where Jesus stopped reading:

*He [God] has sent me [Jesus] to tell those who mourn that **the time of the Lord's favor has come, and with it, the day of God's anger** against their enemies. To all who mourn in Israel, he will give a crown of beauty for ashes, a joyous blessing instead of mourning, festive praise instead of despair. In their righteousness, they will be like great oaks that the Lord has planted for his own glory* (Isaiah 61:2-3).

As a recap of our assignments as illustrated in Isaiah 61, we are to:

- Bring good news to the poor
- Comfort the brokenhearted
- Proclaim that captives will be released
- Proclaim prisoners will be freed
- Comfort all who mourn
- Console those who mourn in Israel
- Give them beauty for ashes
- Give them a joyous blessing instead of mourning
- Give them festive praise instead of despair

Jesus came to save the world from sin. One of the effects of sin is grief. Part of our assignment is to comfort all who mourn. Comfort and restoration is beautifully described in this text. Instead of the ashes of mourning, He gives His people beauty. Instead of the mourning itself, He gives His people a joyous blessing. Instead of the spirit of heaviness (despair), He gives His people festive praise.

Why do we sit in the ashes, why do we mourn, why do we indulge the spirit of heaviness when Jesus gave us so much more and better?

The word "beauty" brings to mind a beautiful crown or head ornament. It is translated "exquisite hats" in Exodus 39:28 (NKJV), and Isaiah 3:20 lists some of the headdresses and decorations that were worn. However, in mourning or times of distress, ashes would be cast upon the head (see 2 Samuel 13:19). Here in Isaiah 61, ashes are replaced with a beautiful crown.

This picture that God is painting through Isaiah 61 brings hope. Verse 3 especially colors our spirits with optimism and expectation:

> To all who mourn in Israel, he will give a crown of beauty for ashes, a joyous blessing instead of mourning, festive praise instead of despair. In their righteousness, they will be like great oaks that the Lord has planted for his own glory (Isaiah 61:3).

The restored place of God's people is glorious. They will become as strong, beautiful, and useful as trees—and not just any trees but righteous ones. And even more wonderful is the fact that, when people look at the trees, they will see that they are the plantings of the Lord.

Oak trees have been a staple tree in many societies for centuries and can live well over 200 years. They provide hundreds of benefits including lumber and food for wildlife, as well as providing shade for tired passersby.

As God's children individually and as His church collectively, we, like the mighty oaks, should be staples in our communities for as long as we live on this earth. We should provide hundreds of benefits to others including encouragement, hope, support, love, as well as providing a place for others to feel safe and secure.

Much of the Bible is written from an agriculture perspective. From the beginning of time, God uses the metaphor of plants and trees to express His human creation. In Psalm 1:3 we read that blessed people are *like trees planted along the riverbank, bearing fruit each season. Their leaves never wither, and they prosper in all they do.*" Another example in the Bible, Psalm 92:12 NIV, expresses that *"The righteous will flourish like a palm tree, they will grow like a cedar of Lebanon."*

Numbers 24:6 says that, *"They spread before me like palm groves, like gardens by the riverside. They are like tall trees planted by the Lord, like cedars beside the waters."* Jeremiah 17:8 also confirms the metaphor, *"They are like trees planted along a riverbank, with roots that reach deep into the water. Such trees are not bothered by the heat or worried by long months of drought. Their leaves stay green, and they never stop producing fruit."*

How deeply rooted are we in the living waters of God's unfailing love? Are we like cedars, strong and healthy? Are we like the grace-full palm trees that bend with the wind but don't break in the storms? Are we like fruit trees that produce fruit without ceasing? God gives us everything we need to be successful in life—in our relationships, our careers, our family. How often do we seek His face first for favor before seeking it from our co-workers, friends, or spouses?

The year of the Lord's favor is a year to claim as your very own. This is the year to acknowledge your relationship with Him. The year to step out and reveal your love for the Lord Jesus Christ. When there is so much trouble and turmoil worldwide—widely caused by religious zealots—now is the time to stand up for what you believe. When challenges come your way, don't shy away from proclaiming that Jesus is Lord of your life; He is your Savior and Redeemer.

The story of American Cassie Rene Bernall still rings in my ears. In 1999, she was the 17-year-old student at Columbine High School in the state of Colorado who stood strong in the face of death to proclaim her God. The following is a report of her death and the incidents leading up to it:

> A born-again Christian as of 1997, Cassie was active in church youth programs and Bible study groups. Her parents called her "Bunny Rabbit" and said she loved to go rock climbing in Breckinridge. She had recently visited Great Britain and her favorite movie was *Braveheart*.[3]

> On April 20, 1999, two teenage gunmen kill 13 people in a shooting spree at Columbine High School in Littleton, Colorado, south of Denver. At approximately 11:19 a.m., Dylan Klebold, 18, and Eric Harris, 17, dressed in trench coats, began

shooting students outside the school before moving inside to continue their rampage. By 11:35 a.m., Klebold and Harris had killed 12 fellow students and a teacher and wounded another 23 people. Shortly after noon, the two teens turned their guns on themselves and committed suicide.

...In the days immediately following the shootings, it was speculated that Klebold and Harris purposely chose jocks, minorities and Christians as their victims. It was initially reported that one student, Cassie Bernall, was allegedly asked by one of the gunmen if she believed in God. When Bernall said, "Yes," she was shot to death. Her parents later wrote a book titled "She Said Yes," honoring their martyred daughter.[4]

For centuries Christians have been persecuted for their faith—from the beginning the devil has been out to destroy God's children. Jesus's disciples died as martyrs, why should we be any different. But would we have the courage to stand up for Him if the time came? Only God knows. We can do our best to read and obey His Word, attend church, show mercy and love—but when the question is asked, "Do you believe in God?" will we shout, "YES!" knowing that He will welcome us with open arms into our eternal, heavenly home.

Remember, even if those who oppose you threaten to destroy you and your God, you can stand firm knowing that no weapon formed against you will succeed. Isaiah 54:17 says it—believe it!

> *But in that coming day no weapon turned against you will succeed. You will silence every voice raised up to accuse you. These benefits are enjoyed by the servants of the Lord; their vindication will come from me. I, the Lord, have spoken!*

Just in case you haven't read Isaiah 61 entirely, or in the New Living Translation, I offer you the remaining verses for you now to enjoy and savor each of the words of hope and promise from the Lord:

> *They will **rebuild the ancient ruins**, repairing cities destroyed long ago. They will **revive them**, though they have been deserted for many generations. **Foreigners will be your servants**. They will feed your flocks and plow*

*your fields and tend your vineyards. **You will be called priests of the Lord,** ministers of our God. **You will feed on the treasures of the nations and boast in their riches.** Instead of shame and dishonor, **you will enjoy a double share of honor. You will possess a double portion of prosperity in your land, and everlasting joy will be yours.***

*For I, the Lord, love justice. I hate robbery and wrongdoing. **I will faithfully reward my people for their suffering** and make an everlasting covenant with them. **Their descendants will be recognized and honored among the nations.** Everyone will realize that **they are a people the Lord has blessed.***

*I am overwhelmed with joy in the Lord my God! For he has **dressed me with the clothing of salvation and draped me in a robe of righteousness.** I am like a bridegroom dressed for his wedding or a bride with her jewels. **The Sovereign Lord will show his justice** to the nations of the world. Everyone will praise him! His righteousness will be like a garden in early spring, with plants springing up everywhere* (Isaiah 61:4-11).

The acceptable year of the Lord, the year of favor, is full of abundant riches. I have highlighted some of the good things we can expect from God when we are obedient and willing to do His will. After all, He knows our past, present, and future—He knows what is best for us and is more than willing to give it to us.

What enemies have destroyed and ruined over the years will be rebuilt. No matter how many mistakes you may have made or relationships were ruined through neglect or abuse or wrong decisions, God will help you rebuild. He will be with you every step of the way. Even if family problems have plagued you for generations, those curses will be destroyed and problems solved.

You probably know the Bible story about the woman caught in adultery. This woman's life was ruined, she was not only caught with a man who was not her husband, she had been with several other men as well.

for you have had five husbands, and you aren't even married to the man you're living with now (John 4:18).

In those days, this woman's life was destroyed, ruined, and many thought her life should be ended, by stoning her to death.

But Jesus! Jesus said to the vengeful crowd, *"He who is without sin among you, let him throw a stone at her first"* (John 8:7 NKJV). The crowd walked away. Then Jesus said to her, *"Neither do I condemn you; go and sin no more."* Then Jesus spoke to them again, saying, *"I am the light of the world. He who follows Me shall not walk in darkness, but have the light of life"* (John 8:11-12 NKJV).

God loves to restore ruins. He wants to use His people to restore and rebuild people and things that are broken down and ruined. Under the empowerment of the Spirit, and the ministry of the Messiah, God's people will be rebuilders. A beautiful example is when Nehemiah took the decades-old rubble of Jerusalem's walls and rebuilt them: *"So on October 2 the wall was finished—just fifty-two days after we had begun. When our enemies and the surrounding nations heard about it, they were frightened and humiliated. They realized this work had been done with the help of our God"* (Nehemiah 6:15-16).

Rather than going alone in life, God will introduce you to people you never knew before and they will help you with your everyday living. Maybe you will be offered a new job with a larger salary. Perhaps you will meet someone who can show you or train you to improve your status in life. God will allow people to enter your life who will feed your soul, plow under your fears, and tend to your concerns. Accept them as gifts from God.

When you move forward in life, as God gives you the resources, skills, and talents, you will gain the ability to bring honor and prosperity and joy into your life and the life of others. Our Lord is a just and fair God who hates stealing and evildoing. He will faithfully reward you for suffering for His namesake. His promises are sure and nations worldwide will realize that you are blessed by the Lord.

You are clothed with salvation and righteousness, dressed to meet your Bridegroom when He comes for you. At that time, you and everyone around the world will praise Him for His righteousness. Hallelujah!

Endnotes

1. Franklin Graham, "The Year of the Lord's Favor," June 12, 2008; http://billygraham. org/story/the-year-of-the-lords-favor/; accessed January 23, 2016.

2. *"that at the name of Jesus every knee should bow..."* (Philippians 2:10).

3. http://acolumbinesite.com/victim/cassie.html; accessed February 17, 2016.

4. http://www.history.com/this-day-in-history/columbine-high-school-massacre; accessed February 17, 2016.

Chapter 9

The Lord's Day of Vengeance

*The Spirit of the Lord God is upon Me, because the Lord has anointed Me to preach good tidings to the poor; He has sent Me to heal the brokenhearted, to proclaim liberty to the captives, and the opening of the prison to those who are bound; to proclaim the acceptable year of the Lord, and **the day of vengeance of our God**...* (Isaiah 61:1-2 NKJV).

Part of our assignment is to announce the Lord's favor, and in addition it is important to note that it is also the day of the Lord's vengeance—the Lord's time for revenge. God promises to avenge His people. Not only in the Old Testament does the Lord proclaim the day of vengeance but also in the New Testament: *"Dear friends, never take revenge. Leave that to the righteous anger of God. For the Scriptures say, 'I will take revenge; I will pay them back,' says the Lord"* (Romans 12:19).

As mere humans with finite knowledge, we must allow the all-knowing and all-righteous Father to avenge His people. We have to acknowledge His superiority in all things and all ways. Only God can mete out the appropriate punishment—or privilege.

Hebrews 12:23-24 says of vengeance:

*You have come to the assembly of God's firstborn children, whose names are written in heaven. You have come to God himself, who is the judge over all things. You have come to the spirits of the righteous ones in heaven who have now been made perfect. **You have come to Jesus, the one who mediates the new covenant between God and people,** and to the sprinkled blood, **which speaks of forgiveness instead of crying out for vengeance** like the blood of Abel.*

No longer are we to seek revenge or vengeance against our enemies. There will come a day—the Lord's day of vengeance—when the God Almighty will demand justice for injustice, punishment for undeserved punishment, and damnation for those who reject Him. Vengeance is God's response to sin and rebellion—God's response, not ours. Although God is amazingly merciful, there comes a time when He demands justice and righteousness—vengeance.

A few examples of God's stand against evil include:

- The worldwide Flood (Genesis 6:17; 7:23)
- Destruction of Sodom and Gomorrah (Genesis 19:24-25)
- Pharaoh's army drowned in the Red Sea (Exodus 15:4)
- Destruction of Babylon (Isaiah 13:1-6)
- Annihilation of the Anakites (Deuteronomy 2:21)
- Baal worshipers (Deuteronomy 4:3)

One of the most descriptive Scripture passages revealing the Lord's vengefulness is found in Isaiah 13:11-13:

*I, the Lord, will punish the world for its evil and the wicked for their sin. I will crush the arrogance of the proud and humble the pride of the mighty. I will make people scarcer than gold—more rare than the fine gold of Ophir. For I will shake the heavens. **The earth will move from its place when the Lord of Heaven's Armies displays his wrath in the day of his fierce anger.***

And Ezra 8:22 states of God's fierce anger:

For I was ashamed to ask the king for soldiers and horsemen to accompany us and protect us from enemies along the way. After all, we had told the king,

*"Our God's hand of protection is on all who worship him, but **his fierce anger** rages against those who abandon him."*

And Lamentations 2:1:

*The Lord in his **anger** has cast a dark shadow over beautiful Jerusalem. The fairest of Israel's cities lies in the dust, thrown down from the heights of heaven. In his day of great **anger**, the Lord has shown no mercy even to his Temple.*

First John 3:8 says:

*But when people keep on sinning, it shows that they belong to the devil, who has been sinning since the beginning. But the Son of God came to **destroy** the works of the devil.*

Jude 1:7:

*And don't forget Sodom and Gomorrah and their neighboring towns, which were filled with immorality and every kind of sexual perversion. Those cities were **destroy**ed by fire and serve as a warning of the eternal fire of God's judgment.*

Revelation 11:18:

*The nations were filled with wrath, but now the time of your wrath has come. It is time to judge the dead and reward your servants the prophets, as well as your holy people, and all who fear your name, from the least to the greatest. It is time to **destroy** all who have caused destruction on the earth.*

John Calvin's commentary on the day of vengeance is interesting to note:

> *For the day of vengeance is in my heart.* In the former clause of this verse Isaiah intimates that God does not cease to discharge his office, though he does not instantly execute his judgments, but, on the contrary, delays till a seasonable time, which he knows well; and that it does not belong to us to prescribe to him when

or how he ought to do this or that, but we ought to bow submissively to his decree, that he may administer all things according to his pleasure. Let us not, therefore, imagine that he is asleep, or that he is idle, when he delays.

Some pastors and scholars say that Revelation 19:11-21 is John's description of the Day of the Lord's Vengeance:

*Then I saw heaven opened, and a white horse was standing there. **Its rider was named Faithful and True, for he judges fairly and wages a righteous war.** His eyes were like flames of fire, and on his head were many crowns. A name was written on him that no one understood except himself. He wore a robe dipped in blood, and **his title was the Word of God.** The armies of heaven, dressed in the finest of pure white linen, followed him on white horses. From his mouth came a sharp sword to strike down the nations. He will rule them with an iron rod. **He will release the fierce wrath of God, the Almighty,** like juice flowing from a winepress. On his robe at his thigh was written this title: **King of all kings and Lord of all lords.***

Then I saw an angel standing in the sun, shouting to the vultures flying high in the sky: "Come! Gather together for the great banquet God has prepared. Come and eat the flesh of kings, generals, and strong warriors; of horses and their riders; and of all humanity, both free and slave, small and great."

*Then I saw the beast and the kings of the world and their armies gathered together to fight against the one sitting on the horse and his army. And the beast was captured, and with him the false prophet who did mighty miracles on behalf of the beast—miracles that deceived all who had accepted the mark of the beast and who worshiped his statue. Both **the beast and his false prophet were thrown alive into the fiery lake of burning sulfur. Their entire army was killed** by the sharp sword that came from the mouth of the one riding the white horse. And the vultures all gorged themselves on the dead bodies.*

Jesus's second coming will be totally unlike His first arrival on earth. This time He comes to destroy evil with all the power of God and the armies of heaven.

Everyone will know who He is and what He came to accomplish. "Vengeance is mine," says the Lord (see Romans 12:19).

ROMANS 12:19 EXPOSED

John Gill's Exposition of the Bible has the following to say about Romans 12:19 (King James Version):

"Dearly beloved"

This affectionate appellation the apostle makes use of, expressing his great love to them, the rather to work upon then, and move them to an attention to what he is about to say; which they might assure themselves was in great tenderness to them, for their good, as well as the glory of God: moreover, he may hereby suggest to them, not only that they were dear to him, but that they were greatly beloved of God, that they were high in his favour and affection; and this he might him unto them, in order to melt them into love to their fellow Christians and fellow creatures, and even to their enemies, and never think of private revenge:

"avenge not yourselves,"

this is no ways contrary to that revenge, a believer has upon sin, and the actings of it, which follows on true evangelical repentance for it, (2 Corinthians 7:11) , and lies in a displicency at it, and himself for it, and in abstaining from it, and fighting against it; nor to that revenge a church may take of the disobedience of impenitent and incorrigible offenders, by laying censures on them, withdrawing from them, and rejecting them from their communion; nor to that revenge which civil magistrates may execute upon them that do evil; but this only forbids and condemns private revenge in private persons, for private injuries done, and affronts given:

"but rather give place unto wrath:"

either to a man's own wrath, stirred up by the provocations given him; let him not rush upon revenge immediately; let him sit down and breathe upon it; let him "give" (arta), "space," unto it, as the Syriac, which may signify time as well as place; and by taking time his wrath will, subside, he will cool and come to himself, and think better on it: or to the wrath of the injurious person, by declining him, as Jacob did Esau, till his wrath was over; or by patiently hearing without resistance the evil done, according to the advice of Christ, (Matthew 5:39 Matthew 5:40); or to the wrath of God, leave all with him, and to the day of his wrath and righteous judgment, who will render to every man according to his works; commit yourselves to him that judgeth righteously, and never think of avenging your own wrongs; and this sense the following words incline to,

for it is written, (Deuteronomy 32:35)

Vengeance is mine, I will repay, saith the Lord;

vengeance belongs to God, and to him only; it is proper and peculiar to him, not to Heathen deities, one of which they call (dikh), "vengeance"; see (Acts 28:4); nor to Satan, who is of a revengeful spirit, and is styled the enemy and the avenger; nor to men, unless to magistrates under God, who are revengers and executioners of his wrath on wicked men; otherwise it solely belongs to God the lawgiver, whose law is broken, and against whom sin is committed: and there is reason to believe he will "repay" it, from the holiness of his nature, the strictness of his justice, his power and faithfulness, his conduct towards his own people, even to his Son, as their surety; nor will he neglect, but in his own time will avenge his elect, which cry unto him day and night; and who therefore should never once think of avenging themselves, but leave it with their God, to whom it belongs.

We must have faith in our loving and merciful Father in Heaven to avenge the wicked. Our spirits and attitudes must reflect love—not revenge or bitterness. Those attributes will destroy us from the inside out. As mere humans we have no idea the best way to mete out justice. Our perspective is so very limited—God's is so very vast. God knows the best time and has the best plan to bring glory to Himself and favor to His righteous children.

Think of those with whom you are angry or bitter. Determine today to forgive them, and then hand them over to God. You can be assured 100 percent that God is the only just avenger. After all, God's law was and is forevermore. God is the lawgiver, the judge and jury—there is none like Him.

We should not pretend to be God and pronounce judgment on people based on our hurt feelings or jealousy or self-righteousness. No. We must do away with our bigotry and self-absorption and allow God to control the situation—every situation. He has the answer to every problem. And so do you—every answer is in the Bible.

OUR BEST EXAMPLE

For example—our best and most wonderful example—Jesus was angry at the people who were gouging people (moneychangers) who were making an exorbitant profit exchanging foreign money for temple coinage. And He was angry at the people who were buying and selling birds and animals for sacrifice in the temple area. Jesus forcefully drove out all those who had desecrated the temple—God's house. He told them, *"It is written [in Scripture], 'My house shall be called a house of prayer'; but you are making it a robbers' den"* (Matthew 21:12-13 AMP).

What can we learn from Jesus' actions? Several lessons:

1. Jesus realized what was going on and knew it was wrong.

2. Jesus took appropriate action to right the wrong.

3. Jesus spoke the Word of God.

Jesus didn't walk into the temple and turn a blind eye to the shenanigans going on. Jesus didn't see what was going on and then turn to His disciples and whine and complain about the problem. Jesus didn't condone what was going on as an act of "tolerance." Jesus didn't try and talk them out of what they were doing. No. Jesus took firm action—without harming anyone—clearly displaying His righteous indignation.

We must have open spiritual eyes to see what's wrong in our relationships, our families, our churches, our communities, and our nations. Then we have to take action to right those wrongs. And most importantly, we must know the Word of God so that all of our actions are based on His righteousness—not our own opinions, wants, desires, or revenge.

Only God's anger is just. Only God's justice is impartial. Only God's vengeance is fair. Knowing that, we can temper our actions and reactions to wrongs. When we seek to right the many wrongs in our society, our motive must be love, not revenge.

Where may your assignment take you? Perhaps into the "temple" (local church) to clean house. Are there programs or ministries that are veering away from the "house of prayer" foundation? Are people buying and selling as if conducting business rather than shepherding people into God's sanctuary? What are the priorities? Are they in line with the Scriptures?

Or perhaps your assignment will take you into the political arena where decisions are made that affect entire communities, regions, or nations. You may be called to influence local elected officials—or become one yourself. You may have an aversion for that type of assignment, but so did Moses...and look at how God used him to save a nation! (See Exodus 4:28.)

Maybe you will be led to participate in your children's school in some way—helping the slower students with math, reading stories, furnishing treats, or providing fun activities. A Christian parent can make a huge difference in a classroom, introducing children to the love and mercy of Jesus by your kind words and actions. Being a role model for youngsters is better than spouting Scripture to cynical adults who tune you out.

As you determine to allow God His vengeance, you can concentrate on sharing all your blessings with others. When you give God His due—rather than trying to keep it for yourself, it frees you to be gracious, tender-hearted, and loving. You can easily reach out to people of all ages and careers and nationalities with a true and pure spirit.

Chapter 10

SET APART FOR GOD'S SERVICE

As we focus on our assignment, the Lord will provide for us in different ways. We will not be encumbered with the everyday pressures of living and doing as normal, God will ensure that we can focus on our assignment in dedicated service to Him. God's people, under the anointing of the Spirit and the ministry of the Messiah, will have a holy occupation. God will provide others to take care of the necessities of life so that the assignment He has given us can be accomplished.

Throughout the Bible God has spoken about His people—you and me—being set apart, special ones whom He cherishes:

And you shall be holy to Me, for I the Lord am holy, and have separated you from the peoples, that you should be Mine (Leviticus 20:26 NKJV).

For you are a holy people to the Lord your God; the Lord your God has chosen you to be a people for Himself, a special treasure above all the peoples on the face of the earth (Deuteronomy 7:6 NKJV).

Also today the Lord has proclaimed you to be His special people, just as He promised you, that you should keep all His commandments, and that He will set you high above all nations which He has made, in praise, in name, and in honor, and that you may be a holy people to the Lord your God, just as He has spoken (Deuteronomy 26:18-19 NKJV).

For now I have chosen and sanctified this house, that My name may be there forever; and My eyes and My heart will be there perpetually (2 Chronicles 7:16 NKJV).

To the church of God which is at Corinth, to those who are sanctified in Christ Jesus, called to be saints, with all who in every place call on the name of Jesus Christ our Lord, both theirs and ours (1 Corinthians 1:2 NKJV).

just as He chose us in Him before the foundation of the world, that we should be holy and without blame before Him in love (Ephesians 1:4 NKJV).

who has saved us and called us with a holy calling, not according to our works, but according to His own purpose and grace which was given to us in Christ Jesus before time began (2 Timothy 1:9 NKJV).

But you are a chosen generation, a royal priesthood, a holy nation, His own special people, that you may proclaim the praises of Him who called you out of darkness into His marvelous light (1 Peter 2:9 NKJV).

Only when we realize how very precious and special we are to God can we become fully alive. Only when we realize how very generous and merciful our God is can we become fully committed to His plan for our lives—our assignment.

God could have seen how good His creation was—the heavens and the earth, day and night, waters and land, birds and beasts, man and woman—and then left it all to fend for itself. But He didn't. He walked with Adam and Eve in the Garden. They enjoyed each other's company and perfect relationship between Creator and the created. God loved His creation so much that He showed the humans mercy over and over again and again. He stayed by them through terrible tragedies that they brought upon themselves.

Generation after generation, people on every continent around the world are at the mercy of an almighty God—thankfully and only by the grace of that almighty God do we exist today.

You are set apart to bring His plan to fruition, to bring the world closer to His glory and His ultimate design that none should perish but rather repent and have eternal life (see John 3:15-16; John 10:28; 2 Peter 3:9 NKJV).

What an amazing God we serve—and should be proud and honored to serve! Every morning when we open our eyes there needs to be songs of praise on our lips and sunshine in our hearts that He has given us another day to live for Him. We are set apart for His service—what a privilege!

THE "WHOLE" PICTURE

Nick Vujicic is a man to admire. He was born without arms and without legs—he was not a "whole" person. As you can well imagine, as a child he struggled mentally and emotionally and physically. Today, at age 34 he is a phenomenal evangelist who speaks worldwide—fulling his assignment. "If just one more person finds eternal life in Jesus Christ...it is all worth it," he says on his Website. If you haven't heard of this remarkable young man, you will find the following information amazing:

> The early days were difficult. Throughout his childhood, Nick not only dealt with the typical challenges of school and adolescence, but he also struggled with depression and loneliness. Nick constantly wondered why he was different than all the other kids. He questioned the purpose of life, or if he even had a purpose.
>
> According to Nick, the victory over his struggles, as well as his strength and passion for life today, can be credited to his faith in God. His family, friends and the many people he has encountered along the journey have inspired him to carry on, as well.
>
> Since his first speaking engagement at age 19, Nick has traveled around the world, sharing his story with millions, sometimes in stadiums filled to capacity, speaking to a range of diverse groups such as students, teachers, young people, business professionals and church congregations of all sizes. Today this dynamic young evangelist has accomplished more than most people achieve in a lifetime. He's an author, musician, actor, and his hobbies include fishing, painting and swimming. In 2007, Nick made the long

journey from Australia to southern California where he is the president of the international non-profit ministry, Life Without Limbs, which was established in 2005.

Nick says, "If God can use a man without arms and legs to be His hands and feet, then He will certainly use any willing heart!" Nick's latest foray into radio will expand his platform for inviting men and women all around the world to embrace the liberating hope and message of Jesus Christ.[1]

Posted on the Life Without Limbs Website is Jeremiah 29:11, *"For I know the plans I have for you,' declares the Lord, 'plans to prosper you and not to harm you, plans to give you hope and a future.'"* Nick also writes there:

Because of the ministry of Life Without Limbs, *God has used me* in countless schools, churches, prisons, orphanages, hospitals, stadiums and in face-to-face encounters with individuals, telling them how very precious they are to God. *It is our greatest pleasure to assure people that God does have a plan for each and every life* that is meaningful and purposeful, for *God took my life, one that others might disregard as not having any significance and He has filled me with His purpose and showed me His plans to use me to move hearts and lives toward Him.*

Does this man who, has raised himself up from legitimate distress and despair to acceptance and action, motivate you to launch yourself into your assignment with gusto? I hope so!

Nick Vujicic's extreme physical condition didn't hold him back from seeking God, seeking God's healing of his mind and emotions, seeking God's purpose, his assignment in life. Only when we too ask, seek, and knock will we receive from God our assignment. God placed a purpose, a unique assignment, inside every person He created.

Pastor Rick Warren authored a popular book a few years ago, *The Purpose Driven Life.* It sold more than 30 million copies. Why? Because people want to know what their purpose is here on earth. They realize that there is "something bigger" than our every day-to-day life—"someOne bigger" they must connect with to become whole.

Are you a whole person today? Have you given your entire being—body, soul, mind, spirit—to God? Or perhaps, like many people, you have pulled out portions of yourself to give to God but keep other areas for yourself. Maybe there is a certain series of books you enjoy reading but the characters and the theme are not righteous or pure or noble or lovely (see Philippians 4:8). Maybe there is a place you like to go with friends where the atmosphere is dark and the conversations are lewd or vulgar. Could there be a relationship that you know deep down is unhealthy for you and the other person but you maintain the connection?

I could write many more examples of ways people keep from giving their entire selves to God—I know many more because I've counseled people near and far about them, and I know personally how easily and quickly we can tuck things, and people, away for our own selfish and fleshly use.

To experience the exciting, joyous, and lovable times God wants for us, these areas of our lives must be:

1. Recognized as ungodly and unhealthy

2. Repented of and ask God for forgiveness

3. Dealt with as quickly as possible

4. Totally turned over to the Holy Spirit to destroy

5. Rooted out and the void filled with godly and healthy thoughts and actions

You will receive the strength and empowerment to do what needs to be done when you sincerely ask God to forgive and anoint you. After all, you *are* set apart to fulfill your assignment, so of course God will provide you with what you need to become holy—as He is holy.

> So **prepare your minds for action and exercise self-control. Put all your hope in the gracious salvation** that will come to you when Jesus Christ is revealed to the world. So **you must live as God's obedient children. Don't slip back into your old ways of living to satisfy your own desires.** You didn't know any better then. But **now you must be holy in everything you do**, just as **God** who **chose you** is holy. For the Scriptures say, "You must be holy because I am holy" (1 Peter 1:13-16).

HOLY, NOT SELF-RIGHTEOUS

I have no doubt you know people who act "self-righteous"—and they are not pleasant people to be around. They seem to think that their way is the only way to be a Christian. They follow certain rules and don't do certain things or say certain words.

The Merriam-Webster Dictionary's definition of self-righteous is: Having or showing a strong belief that your own actions, opinions, etc., are right and other people's are wrong; convinced of one's own righteousness especially in contrast with the actions and beliefs of others; narrow-mindedly moralistic.

Yup, I bet several people came to your mind while reading that definition. But did your own reflection come to your mind? It is not hard to fall into a self-righteous mode after becoming a Christian. We can put ourselves above others—when Jesus did the exact opposite. We can think ourselves better because we no longer cuss or steal or slander or covet or murder or any of the "Big 10." But are we really being honest with ourselves or with God?

How about the times when we "think" a cuss word at the person who just cut us off in traffic, or take home from work some office supplies, or gossip about someone at church—murdering that person's character.

Jesus, our Ultimate Role Model, thought of Himself as a servant, lesser than others. He took it upon Himself to wash the feet of His disciples—whether they deserved His kindness or not, He performed the act many of us would cringe at doing (see John 13:5-17 NKJV).

> *After washing their feet, he* [Jesus] *put on his robe again and sat down and asked, "Do you understand what I was doing? You call me 'Teacher' and 'Lord,' and you are right, because that's what I am. And since I, your Lord and Teacher, have washed your feet, you ought to wash each other's feet. I have given you an example to follow. Do as I have done to you. I tell you the truth, slaves are not greater than their master. Nor is the messenger more important than the one who sends the message. Now that you know these things, God will bless you for doing them* (John 13:12-17).

Another Scripture comes to mind, Philippians 2:3: *"Don't be selfish; don't try to impress others. Be humble, thinking of others as better than yourselves."* Yes, this is the attitude of a truly mature Christian. When we are devoted to Christ our Lord, we will not be selfish or try to impress others, rather we will be humble and contrite in our dealings with others.

Can we be totally unselfish 24-7? Sorry to say, no. Because we are human and "works in progress," we will have moments when selfishness and arrogance will rise up within us. BUT, because we are living for the Lord, the Holy Spirit within us will prick our consciences, our spirits, and we will realize our sin and repent of it. We will apologize if necessary to the person or rectify the situation as quickly as possible.

Therefore, the key is that we must listen for, acknowledge, and then be obedient to the still, small Voice, the Holy Spirit, who is pricking our spirit, our inner self. He is our Guiding Light within, keeping us on the right track, out of trouble, and clearing the way for us to move forward into maturity. Jesus said, *"But the Helper, the Holy Spirit, whom the Father will send in My name, He will teach you all things, and bring to your remembrance all things that I said to you"* (John 14:26 NKJV).

When the Holy Spirit brings to our remembrance, He is delivering a message to your inner self that reminds you of what you read in God's Word, what the pastor preached last week or last month, what your parents taught you about Jesus when you were a child, etc. The Holy Spirit is a perfect record keeper who enables you to remember what is right and wrong, good and bad—godly and ungodly.

How many times have you been in an awkward situation or faced a challenging circumstance and you were at a loss what to do next, when suddenly a thought enters your mind that totally solves the problem? If you are tuned in to the Holy Spirit, He will prevent you from becoming a self-righteous, arrogant Christian snob. That type of person turns off others from Christianity rather than attracting others to Him.

HUMBLE, NOT UNDULY COMPLIANT

Being humble doesn't mean you are a doormat for aggressive or more assertive people. Being humble doesn't mean you are to go along with others who are not going in the "right" direction. Being humble doesn't mean allowing a bully to change your mind about important issues—especially your faith and beliefs.

Being humble doesn't mean you are a wimp.

Humbleness means you are free from pride and arrogance. Just as Jesus knew, you know that in yourself you can do nothing (see John 5:30). Being humble means that you know who you are in Christ, that He is your Savior, your Deliverer. Jesus was and is a humble Man of God and you are privileged to emulate Him.

Like being "set apart" is prevalent throughout the Old and New Testaments, so is being humble noted Bible-wide. A few examples of how important humbleness is to God are cited for your consideration and meditation:

Humble yourselves before the Lord, and he will lift you up in honor (James 4:10).

You [God] rescue the humble, but your eyes watch the proud and humiliate them (2 Samuel 22:28).

The humble will see their God at work and be glad. Let all who seek God's help be encouraged (Psalm 69:32).

The Lord mocks the mockers but is gracious to the humble (Proverbs 3:34).

Human pride will be brought down, and human arrogance will be humbled. Only the Lord will be exalted on that day of judgment (Isaiah 2:17).

The humble will be filled with fresh joy from the Lord. The poor will rejoice in the Holy One of Israel (Isaiah 29:19).

Seek the Lord, all who are humble, and follow his commands. Seek to do what is right and to live humbly. Perhaps even yet the Lord will protect you—protect you from his anger on that day of destruction (Zephaniah 2:3).

Take my yoke upon you. Let me teach you, because I am humble and gentle at heart, and you will find rest for your souls (Matthew 11:29).

Always be humble and gentle. Be patient with each other, making allowance for each other's faults because of your love (Ephesians 4:2).

Finally, all of you should be of one mind. Sympathize with each other. Love each other as brothers and sisters. Be tenderhearted, and keep a humble attitude (1 Peter 3:8).

ENDNOTE

1.   http://www.lifewithoutlimbs.org/about-nick/bio/; accessed January 25, 2016.

Chapter 11

Rejoicing in God's Great Blessings

Instead of shame and dishonor, you will enjoy a double share of honor.
You will possess a double portion of prosperity in your land, and
everlasting joy will be yours (Isaiah 61:7).

A dramatic change in our circumstances will take place when we walk in our assignment:

- No more shame or dishonor

- No more confusion

- No more despair

- We shall receive a double share of honor

- We shall be happy with a double share of prosperity

- We will experience joy that never ends and cannot be taken away

God's blessings are ours for the asking. As discussed previously, we have only to ask, seek, and knock and God will shower us with all that is good. Blessings come in a million different ways and forms. I have no doubt that you can quickly name ten blessings that God has given you.

The first ten blessings that come to my mind right now:

1. Jesus, the greatest blessing of all
2. Living in a country where I can openly worship God
3. The Bible, God's Word, and my ability to read, write, and learn
4. My wife and children
5. The air I am breathing
6. Good health and a sound mind
7. My eyes and ears to see and hear all of God's creations
8. Walking in my God-given assignment
9. Our great church family
10. Our home that provides shelter, warmth, and food

The Lord explains in detail the blessings we will receive if we are obedient to Him and keep all of His commands—which we are willing to do when we are walking forward into maturity while fulfilling our assignments:

> *If you fully obey the Lord your God and carefully keep all his commands that I am giving you today, the Lord your God will* **set you high above all the nations** *of the world.* **You will experience all these blessings** *if you obey the Lord your God: Your* **towns and your fields will be blessed.** *Your* **children and your crops will be blessed.**
>
> *The* **offspring of your herds and flocks will be blessed.** *Your* **fruit baskets and breadboards will be blessed.** *Wherever you go and whatever you do, you will be blessed.*
>
> *The* **Lord will conquer your enemies** *when they attack you. They will attack you from one direction, but they will scatter from you in seven!*
>
> *The* **Lord will guarantee a blessing on everything you do** *and will fill your storehouses with grain. The Lord* **your God will bless you** *in the land he is giving you.*

*If you obey the commands of the Lord your God and walk in his ways, **the Lord will establish you as his holy people** as he swore he would do. Then all the nations of the world will see that **you are a people claimed by the Lord**, and they will stand in awe of you.*

***The Lord will give you prosperity** in the land he swore to your ancestors to give you, **blessing you with many children, numerous livestock, and abundant crops. The Lord will send rain** at the proper time from his rich treasury in the heavens and will **bless all the work you do**. You will lend to many nations, but **you will never need to borrow** from them.*

*If you listen to these commands of the Lord your God that I am giving you today, and if you carefully obey them, **the Lord will make you the head and not the tail**, and **you will always be on top** and never at the bottom. You must not turn away from any of the commands I am giving you today, nor follow after other gods and worship them* (Deuteronomy 28:1-14).

I believe that all of those blessings translate into modern-day terms as:

Living out your assignment can bring you before nations—people around the world will notice you because you are reaching out to them via the Internet or other means to share the Good News. Because you are obeying God, your community and workplace will experience blessings, as will your children and the fruits of your labors. Your business or place of work will be blessed because the anointing is being revealed through you to others. You will not go hungry or be in need of food—the Lord will provide for your physical needs. Wherever you go and whatever you do for God's glory, He will bless you doubly.

When adversaries at home or work or even church attack you, they will be shut down by the mighty hand of God, scattering them afar. He will allow others to see you as He sees you—a special, holy person set apart for use by the Lord. You will have a home with children and a joyful life of abundance. God will shower you not only with rain to nourish your physical land to make the grass and trees and flowers grow, God's showers of blessings will also bring success in your work, your relationships, your spiritual life, your finances, and every aspect of your daily living.

*The godly are **showered with blessings**...* (Proverbs 10:6).

But it will go well for those who convict the guilty; ***rich blessings will be showered on them*** (Proverbs 24:25).

I will bless my people and their homes around my holy hill. And in the proper season I will send the showers they need. ***There will be showers of blessing*** (Ezekiel 34:26).

If you don't read the Bible and don't meditate on the beautiful words in His Love Letter, you will never know all of the promises that He makes concerning His children—you and me. Who wouldn't want to be showered with blessings? I don't know anyone who would turn down success, abundant resources, food, clothing—every necessity and more! All we have to do is obey God and ask in Jesus's name. When you are a maturing Christian, there will be no problem obeying God, as this is part of your assignment in life. You will *desire* to follow His will for you, because you *know* that it is better than anything you could ever come up with yourself!

No Shame, Dishonor, Confusion, Despair

Have you ever felt ashamed, dishonored, confused, and desperate? Yes, of course you have. Everyone has at one time or another—it's part of life here on earth. (Hallelujah that in Heaven we will cease to experience these types of feelings!)

Adam and Eve, the very first human beings, *"felt no shame"* (Genesis 2:25) when walking together naked in the Garden. They were happy and full of excitement as they enjoyed every moment of every day in the place of perfect harmony between God and His beautiful, pure creation. After they disobeyed God, *"they suddenly felt shame at their nakedness"* (Genesis 3:7).

So from the very beginning of earthly time, shame has plagued humankind. Throughout the Bible there are many instances of people committing shameful acts, others who bring shame to their family or to God. David refers to shame and dishonor numerous times in the book of Psalms, as does Solomon in the book of Proverbs. The New Testament is not without its *"shameful deeds and underhanded methods"* (2 Corinthians 4:2).

It is worthy to note that people without the Holy Spirit to guide them and prick their spirits about what is right and wrong are ungodly and *"have no sense of shame. They live for lustful pleasure and eagerly practice every kind of impurity"* (Ephesians 4:19; also see Romans 1:24-27). May this never be said of us!

If someone is convicted of a disobedience in the military, that person is dishonorably discharged from the service. The person brought dishonor to the military and to him or herself. We should be very careful not to bring dishonor to ourselves, our families, our churches, and especially we should never bring dishonor to our heavenly Father. He is willing to forgive, yet we should never have to ask forgiveness for bringing shame to Him because of our actions or words. God deserves only our utmost respect and humble appreciation for His mighty goodness, faithfulness, and for who He is—God Almighty, Maker of Heaven and earth.

> *They must be set apart as holy to their God and must never bring shame on the name of God. They must be holy, for they are the ones who present the special gifts to the Lord...* (Leviticus 21:6).

As we advance in fulfilling our assignments, let us always be aware of our great responsibility of being ambassadors for Christ. May we realize that people are watching our actions and reactions to situations—good and bad. Do we always give God credit for the good in our lives? We should! And do we accept responsibility for our own mistakes and wrong decisions when bad things happen? We must not take credit for the good and blame God for the bad. No. This is not right. We should know better. Let us acknowledge His goodness and grace at all times—this shines His light on all who hear us and are watching us.

DOUBLE HONOR, PROSPERITY, JOY

No doubt you know the definition of honor, but let's review it again according to the Merriam-Webster dictionary: "respect that is given to someone who is admired; a good reputation; good quality or character as judged by other people; high moral standards of behavior." Also, "good name or public esteem; a person of superior standing; one whose worth brings respect or fame."

Double honor, of course, would be those definitions times two! Therefore, a person of double honor would be one who is greatly sought-after, a superstar, so to speak. God's anointing allows us to become honorable people whom others will respect and admire. We cannot achieve honor and respectability depending on our own whims and desires—only God's grace and mercy and the indwelling of the Holy Spirit can transform people others will want to know and emulate.

When people are honorably discharged from military service, they are held in high regard by all. When applying for a job, their laudable military service benefits them in the decision by employers. When we serve honorably in God's army, He will shower us with benefits beyond our imagination—including prosperity and success.

> *...there will be heard once more the sounds of joy and laughter. The joyful voices of bridegrooms and brides will be heard again, along with the joyous songs of people bringing thanksgiving offerings to the Lord. They will sing, "Give thanks to the Lord of Heaven's Armies, for the Lord is good. His faithful love endures forever!" For I will restore the prosperity of this land to what it was in the past, says the Lord* (Jeremiah 33:10-11).

Prosperity means to prosper—which can point to prosperity in finances, career, health, relationships, etc. To be prosperous is usually associated with financial wealth. While God is certainly not against His people being prosperous financially, He is more than willing and able to grant prosperity in *all* areas of life. For example, Solomon asked God not for gold and wealth but for wisdom. From wisdom, Solomon gained more riches than anyone, ever.

When asking, seeking, and knocking, we must use all of the knowledge that we gain from reading and absorbing His Word so we too, like Solomon, can be as prosperous as God wants us to be. In fact, because we know *all* of Solomon's story, we can be even more wise and prosperous—because we won't be trapped by lust like he was, which led to his downfall (see 1 Kings 11).

There are many true stories about how lottery winners of large sums of money either quickly or eventually lose all their winnings. They were not prepared for the overwhelming temptations that come with financial prosperity.

An article in *Fortune* magazine, written a few days after three people won $1.6 billion, reveals:

Indeed, 44% of those who have ever won large lottery prizes were broke within five years, according to a 2015 Camelot Group study. The Certified Financial Planner Board of Standards says nearly a third declared bankruptcy—meaning they were worse off than before they became rich. Other studies show that lottery winners frequently become estranged from family and friends, and incur a greater incidence of depression, drug and alcohol abuse, divorce, and suicide than the average American.[1]

Have you ever dreamed of winning the lottery? What would you do with all that money? Would you buy all the "stuff" you've wanted over the years, thinking it would make you happy? Luxury home(s), exotic cars, faraway vacations? Or would you be talked into investments that may or may not be profitable. Or how about donating to charities, church ministries, missionaries? Would you tithe 10 percent to your church?

I encourage you to write 10 things you would do with $10 million. Then consider each of those things with the admonitions in God's Word. For example:

Their riches will not last, and their wealth will not endure. Their possessions will no longer spread across the horizon. Let them no longer fool themselves by trusting in empty riches, for emptiness will be their only reward (Job 15:29,31).

Riches won't help on the day of judgment, but right living can save you from death (Proverbs 11:4).

Choose a good reputation over great riches; being held in high esteem is better than silver and gold (Proverbs 22:1).

The trustworthy person will get a rich reward, but a person who wants quick riches will get into trouble (Proverbs 28:20).

We all come to the end of our lives as naked and empty-handed as on the day we were born. We can't take our riches with us (Ecclesiastes 5:15).

Our hearts ache, but we always have joy. We are poor, but we give spiritual riches to others. We own nothing, and yet we have everything (2 Corinthians 6:10).

After reading these few Scripture verses (there are many more throughout the Bible about wealth and riches), would you make any changes on your list of how you would spend $10 million?

These are tough questions, but I believe in preaching real-life scenarios and stirring up minds and spirits to delve deeply into who we truly are. There are no right or wrong answers, as every person who reads this book is at a different, unique place and time in life—each of us is at a different level of spiritual maturity. God holds each of us accountable for what we do with our resources at any given time. Our motivation is key.

Jesus sat down near the collection box in the Temple and watched as the crowds dropped in their money. Many rich people put in large amounts. Then a poor widow came and dropped in two small coins. Jesus called his disciples to him and said, "I tell you the truth, this poor widow has given more than all the others who are making contributions. For they gave a tiny part of their surplus, but she, poor as she is, has given everything she had to live on" (Mark 12:41-44).

I didn't add this Bible passage to make you feel guilty, just to make you think about what is important—really important—in life. People in the "Western" world are rich compared to people living in countries that are less developed. We "Westerners" are able to give of our wealth—and we do. In the United States in the year 2014, total giving to charitable organizations was $358 billion—an increase of 7.1 percent from giving in 2013.[2] "...in 2014, donations from individuals account for roughly 75% of all donations. If you add in gifts from bequests and family foundations, which are essentially gifts from individuals, then the category accounts for nearly 90% of all giving. In other words, the donating public, not big foundations or corporations, is responsible for the vast majority of annual donations."[3]

As "beauty is in the eye of the beholder" so is prosperity. Like millions of people worldwide, you may be a fan of the "fast food" sold under the "golden arches"—but did you know that:

> In 1998, Mrs. Joan Kroc, widow of McDonald's founder Ray Kroc, donated $90 million to The Salvation Army to build a comprehensive community center in San Diego, California.
>
> ...When Mrs. Kroc passed away in October 2003, *she left $1.5 billion*—much of her estate—*to The Salvation Army, by far the largest charitable gift ever given to the Army, and the largest single gift given to any single charity at one time.*
>
> The gift, which eventually grew to $1.8 billion, was split evenly among the four Army Territories—Central, East, South and West. Half of the money was designated to build a series of state-of-the-art Salvation Army Ray and Joan Kroc Corps Community Centers nationwide patterned after the San Diego center, and the other half formed endowments to supplement local fundraising for the centers' ongoing operational costs.
>
> No other U.S. charity has ever undertaken such a sweeping fundraising or construction effort with the potential to impact so many people. By late 2014, 26 Kroc Centers had opened and were serving well over *130,000 people each week*, and growing.[4]

These large dollar numbers are beyond most of our imaginations—I know they are beyond mine. Yet the Lord sees every penny, and the motivation behind each cent donated.

We are to give with a cheerful countenance, *"Give generously to the poor, not grudgingly, for the Lord your God will bless you in everything you do"* (Deuteronomy 15:10). Apostle Paul wrote to the church in Corinth: *"You must each decide in your heart how much to give. And don't give reluctantly or in response to pressure. 'For God loves a person who gives cheerfully'"* (2 Corinthians 9:7).

We are to be generous not only with our financial resources but whatever we have that will aid someone else. For instance:

- Rahab hid in her home the two Israelite spies that Joshua sent to scout out the land on the other side of the Jordan River, around Jericho (see Joshua 2:1-24).

- The Samaritan who gave aid and comfort to the man who was beaten and robbed (see Luke 10:25-37).

- The woman who anointed Jesus with her beautiful alabaster jar of expensive perfume (see Matthew 26:7).

- The woman who gave Elijah her last piece of bread (1 Kings 17:10-12 NKJV).

- Wise men from the East gave the Christ Child gold, frankincense, and myrrh (Matthew 2:10-11 NKJV).

- The Man, Jesus, gave the best wine to wedding guests (John 2:1-10 NKJV).

- Peter gave a healing touch, *"Silver and gold I do not have, but what I do have I give you: In the name of Jesus Christ of Nazareth, rise up and walk"* (Acts 3:6 NKJV).

- Mary and Martha gave hospitality, providing dinner for Jesus (see Luke 10:38-42 NKJV).

- Joseph from Arimathea gave a tomb into which was laid the body of the crucified Jesus (see Luke 23:50-55 NKJV).

Of course there are many other examples in the Bible and hopefully you can think of modern-day examples of people who are giving of their talents, skills, time, effort, and a myriad of resources to aid others—revealing to them the compassion of Christians, followers of the One who gave His life as our Redeeming Savior.

Endnotes

1. Ric Edelman, "Why So Many Lottery Winners Go Broke," *Fortune Insider,* January 15, 2016; http://fortune.com/2016/01/15/powerball-lottery-winners/; accessed January 25, 2016.

2. www.charitynavigator.org/index.cfm?bay=content.view&cpid=42#.VqjwIDHSmM8; accessed January 27, 2016.

3. Ibid.

4. http://www.salvationarmyusa.org/usn/kroc-centers; accessed January 27, 2016.

Conclusion

WHAT WILL
YOU DO NEXT?

Part of our assignment is *to rebuild what is ruined.* Note the words in Isaiah 61:4 (AMP):

Then they will rebuild the ancient ruins, they will raise up and restore the former desolations; and they will renew the ruined cities, the desolations (deserted settlements) of many generations.

Many times people become so discouraged with the problems in their lives that we think there is no way out—that we are destined and doomed to remain in a world of ruin. When we see broken relationships, fractured families, traumatized teenagers, splintered churches, stalled careers, cracked marriages, emotionally injured co-workers, shattered dreams, battered spirits, and the like, we either rise above the fray or we sink beneath it—eventually drowning in our own self-pity or succumbing to physical ailments brought on by our self-made suffering.

We—you and me—have many choices to make every day: whether to rise above a person's unkind comment or sulk about it for days; whether to accept the challenge of a new job or continue to complain about the one we have; whether to lend a hand to someone in need or walk by pretending we don't see.

WHAT NEXT?

What is the next right thing to do? Asking ourselves this question puts us in control mode, which moves us forward. Moving forward is always a good thing. If we stay in one place too long we become useless, unproductive, and unhappy.

A portion of John Gill's Exposition of the Bible says the following about Isaiah 61:4:

> What is here said was literally true, when the Jews returned from Babylon, and built their ruined houses and cities; or, at least, there is an allusion to it: but it respects either the setting up of the interest of Christ, and forming churches in the Gentile world, where nothing but blindness and ignorance reigned; where there were no preaching nor ordinances, but all things were in ruin and confusion; as they were before the ministry of the Gospel by the apostles, who were wise master builders, and instruments of converting multitudes, and of raising churches to the honour of the great Redeemer there: or rather it respects the building up of the tabernacle of David, that is fallen down, or the church of God among the Jews, which will be in the latter day, when they are turned to the Lord, (Amos 9:11) and the same sense have all the following expressions, *they shall raise up the former desolations, and they shall repair the waste cities, the desolations of many generations*; setting forth the desolate state and condition of the Jews; their long continuance in it, age after age; and their recovery and restoration, when they shall become a flourishing people again, both in civil and spiritual things.

I must say that is one of the longest sentences I have ever read. Taking it apart reveals some aspects of Isaiah 61:4 that we may have not considered previously. For instance, after the Jews returned from their captivity in Babylon, the next right thing to do—their first task was to rebuild their houses and cities. They needed shelter from the elements and refuge from their enemies. They would restore the areas in and around the cities, bringing life in forms of trees and crops and the like. Once again the land would overflow with God's goodness and the people would be free from mourning and despair. They would see His splendor in all the plantings that would spring forth.

As the physical rebuilding progressed so would the spiritual rebuilding. Jesus said He was anointed to proclaim the Good News—He read a portion of Isaiah 61 in the Temple for all to hear, so all would know that He is the Messiah. He would be providing hope for the brokenhearted and freedom for the captives. He was proclaiming the day of the Lord's favor and the day of vengeance of God Almighty.

These formerly brokenhearted, mournful, desperate, and poor captives would soon be rebuilding their ruined cities as well as rebuilding ruined generations of families and friends through receiving the Lord's favor.

Jesus is reading Scriptures written in the past to foretell the future. Our God is an amazing God who confounds and comforts us with His wisdom and mercy. When we seriously consider all that He shares with us in His Word, we realize that He holds very little back from us. His wisdom is ours to accept. That is why every time we read the Bible, we receive more and more knowledge. What one verse meant yesterday to us in that moment's situation may mean something else to us next week as we face another situation. God's Word *never* changes, but our application of His Word to our lives constantly changes to fulfill His promises for us.

When we read the prophetic books like Isaiah, we must never think that its interpretation is only for the present. Anything prophetic always takes us into three dimensions—past, present, and future. The book of Isaiah is a historical book, which is past. It is also a book that brings us into the present-day world that is relevant for our daily walk—but it is also a book that foretells the future. Because it's a book of prophecy, it is timeless. The words will always be relative no matter what time or season you are in.

We serve a living God and God's Word is living—it isn't a book of dead words that have no meaning. No. The Scriptures are alive, boldly revealing God Himself within every believer who allows the Holy Spirit to illuminate the mysteries and modalities, the truth and timeliness of every word.

From rebuilding houses and churches and walls and storehouses and vineyards and gardens, God also gives to His children the wherewithal to rebuild relationships and families and teenagers and careers and churches and marriages and dreams and spirits. God says in Amos 9:11, *"In that day I will restore the fallen house of David. I will repair its damaged walls. From the ruins I will rebuild it and restore its former glory."* From the ruins God's glory will rise and shine!

No more will others look upon the rubble and laugh or jeer. No. We, His children who have taken some hard hits from the world, will rise and shine again as the Lord gives us strength and perseverance. People will want to be like us because there will be something special flowing from our hearts and minds and lips. Our words will be *"sweeter than honey"* (Psalm 119:103), dripping with encouragement, hope, and life-changing truth. We will be known for our kind words that are *"sweet to the soul and healthy for the body"* (Proverbs 16:24).

So what we need to do next is the next right thing—which centers on God's Word and our assignment from Him:

- *Read* God's Word daily.

- *Meditate* on each verse, allowing the Holy Spirit to show you the meaning.

- *Follow* His direction that is revealed to you in His Word.

- *Ask* for God's anointing; *seek* your assignment; *knock* on every door of opportunity.

- *Reach out* with love and compassion to people He puts in your path.

- *Share* good tidings and the Good News of the Gospel with everyone.

- *Realize* that you are set apart for God's use and service—and *accept* your assignment.

- *Rejoice* in all the great blessings showered on you by your heavenly Father.

I firmly believe that this is the year of the Lord's favor and we are the ones who will make the difference in God's Kingdom advancement. You are a key player in the ultimate plan of redemption for God's people. Jesus's return is imminent and He is expecting a bride who is ready for marriage to the King of kings and Lord of lords.

In anticipation of His return and the day of vengeance, it is wise to carefully review Jesus's Parable of the Ten Bridesmaids as told in Matthew 25:

Then the Kingdom of Heaven will be like ten bridesmaids who took their lamps and went to meet the bridegroom. Five of them were foolish, and five were wise. The five who were foolish didn't take enough olive oil for their lamps, but the other five were wise enough to take along extra oil. When the bridegroom was delayed, they all became drowsy and fell asleep.

At midnight they were roused by the shout, "Look, the bridegroom is coming! Come out and meet him!" All the bridesmaids got up and prepared their lamps. Then the five foolish ones asked the others, "Please give us some of your oil because our lamps are going out." But the others replied, "We don't have enough for all of us. Go to a shop and buy some for yourselves."

But while they were gone to buy oil, the bridegroom came. Then those who were ready went in with him to the marriage feast, and the door was locked. Later, when the other five bridesmaids returned, they stood outside, calling, "Lord! Lord! Open the door for us!" But he called back, "Believe me, I don't know you!"

So you, too, must keep watch! For you do not know the day or hour of my return (Matthew 25:1-13).

This parable describes Jesus Christ as the Bridegroom and His return for His Bride—the Church. Some were ready to greet Him, others were not. Although we do not know when He will return (even He doesn't know) we are told to be ready. Jesus tells us in Mark 13:32-37:

However, no one knows the day or hour when these things will happen, not even the angels in heaven or the Son himself. Only the Father knows. And since you don't know when that time will come, be on guard! Stay alert! The coming of the Son of Man can be illustrated by the story of a man going on a long trip. When he left home, he gave each of his slaves instructions about the work they were to do, and he told the gatekeeper to watch for his return. You, too, must keep watch! For you don't know when the master of the household will return—in the evening, at midnight, before dawn, or at daybreak. Don't let him find you sleeping when he arrives without warning. I say to you what I say to everyone: Watch for him!

So does this mean we should stop our work or our tending to business or caring for our families and stare out the window, watching for the return of Jesus?

No. We are to go about our daily lives but with our spiritual ears and eyes always alert and ready to welcome Him—our Bridegroom. We must have "oil for our lamps" and "stay awake"—spiritually, so we don't miss our Lord's arrival.

I've always been troubled by the fact that Jesus's disciples couldn't stay awake even for an hour while Jesus was praying, facing His crucifixion—calling out to His Father as His *"soul is crushed with grief to the point of death."* All Jesus asked was for them to, *"Stay here and keep watch with me."* But they let Him down—not once or twice but three times.

> *Then Jesus went with them to the olive grove called Gethsemane, and he said, "Sit here while I go over there to pray." He took Peter and Zebedee's two sons, James and John, and he became anguished and distressed. He told them, "My soul is crushed with grief to the point of death. Stay here and keep watch with me."*
>
> *He went on a little farther and bowed with his face to the ground, praying, "My Father! If it is possible, let this cup of suffering be taken away from me. Yet I want your will to be done, not mine."*
>
> *Then he returned to the disciples and found them asleep. He said to Peter, "Couldn't you watch with me even one hour? Keep watch and pray, so that you will not give in to temptation. For the spirit is willing, but the body is weak!"*
>
> *Then Jesus left them a second time and prayed, "My Father! If this cup cannot be taken away unless I drink it, your will be done." When he returned to them again, he found them sleeping, for they couldn't keep their eyes open.*
>
> *So he went to pray a third time, saying the same things again. Then he came to the disciples and said, "Go ahead and sleep. Have your rest. But look—the time has come. The Son of Man is betrayed into the hands of sinners. Up, let's be going. Look, my betrayer is here!"* (Matthew 26:36-46)

We cannot allow ourselves to sleep through the most important time of our lives—possibly the most important time in history. Of course our physical bodies need sleep and rest, but our spiritual selves must be willing to stay awake and alert—waiting to welcome Jesus our Savior in any way or time He chooses to appear to us.

Are we engaged in fleshly foolishness rather than focusing on what is godly and righteous? Are we concerned more about who is wearing what or driving what than building our faith by reading the Word and focusing on the wisdom found there?

Jesus said, *"Up, let's be going. Look, my betrayer is here!"* We must get up and keep up our guard lest the devil sneak in and distract us from what is most important.

> *And even as Jesus said this, Judas, one of the twelve disciples, arrived with a crowd of men armed with swords and clubs. They had been sent by the leading priests and elders of the people. The traitor, Judas, had given them a pre-arranged signal: "You will know which one to arrest when I greet him with a kiss." So Judas came straight to Jesus. "Greetings, Rabbi!" he exclaimed and gave him the kiss* (Matthew 26:47-49).

Jesus knew who would betray Him. We don't always know who is our enemy and who is our friend. But the Holy Spirit within us will signal us with the truth. We must be awake and alert to hear His still, small voice and His gentle prodding. We must be willing to follow Jesus's lead and pray to our heavenly Father when the world is crashing and thrashing around us. Jesus was the Son of the Almighty God, yet He knew He needed to pray to His Father for strength and stamina for what awaited Him.

How much more do we need to pray to our Father in Heaven for strength and stamina! We are mere humans in a world of chaos and carnality, easily ruled by our flesh and distracted by evil lurking around every corner.

Yet...we are more than conquerors!

> *Yet in all these things **we are more than conquerors through Him who loved us**. For I am persuaded that neither death nor life, nor angels nor principalities nor powers, nor things present nor things to come, nor height nor depth, nor any other created thing, shall be able to separate us from **the love of God** which is in Christ Jesus our Lord* (Romans 8:37-39 NKJV).

We can face anything and anyone because nothing can separate us from the love of God. And now we are back to the main thrust of this book—LOVE. With love all things are possible, all things are lovely, and all people are loveable. Chapter 2 discussed thoroughly why love is so important; perhaps it is best to reread that chapter and let those Scriptures become one with your spirit.

ABOUT THE AUTHOR

Bishop John Francis challenges the Body of Christ to shake off complacency and live as God intended—fruitful and effective. He is uncompromising and means serious business for God. As a result, he is always in great demand for preaching engagements, as well as imparting ministerial advice and spiritual wisdom through the covering he offers pastors as part of his established Ruach Network of Churches.

Bishop John and Co-Pastor Penny Francis are the founders of the United Kingdom's premier Christian TV, "Flow TV," and launched their new station in March 2014, "Bringing Hope, Inspiring Change."

Operating in his gift as an apostle and speaking with a prophetic voice, Bishop Francis is the founder and senior pastor of Ruach City Church—one church in several locations (Brixton in South London; Kilburn in North London; Walthamstow in East London, Birmingham, UK, and Philadelphia in the United States). Ruach City Church is one of the largest and fastest growing churches in the UK. Starting from humble beginnings, with only eighteen faithful members, the church has grown rapidly and continues to grow. Several services are held every Sunday at several locations with more than 8,000+ people in regular attendance.

Bishop John Francis's outreach ministries are many, including his role as international director of the Ruach Network of Churches, overseeing approximately 50 churches in the UK and overseas. In 2012, Ruach City Church launched *Ruach Radio* via Internet (www.ruachradio.com) and can also be heard London-wide on DAB Radio.

A recipient of the British Gospel Association's Award, *Contribution to Gospel Music* and *Gospel TV Series of the Year* (as co-presenter of the UK's pioneering Gospel TV program, *People Get Ready!*), Bishop Francis is a multitalented, multifaceted man of God. He has performed in the presence of Her Majesty, the Queen, the Prince and late Princess of Wales, as well as toured throughout Europe presenting musical workshops and television and radio shows with renowned The Inspirational Choir (UK).

Bishop Francis was awarded the Minister of the Year Oasis Award and Church of the Year Oasis Award; and the Bishop Francis Choir—The Ruach City Church Choir and Musicians recorded on the *Donnie McClurkin "Live in London" Album,* which has now reached platinum level sales—reaching multiple thousands of souls.

Bishop Francis's ministry is local, national, and international with more than 126 million viewers in the USA watching his broadcast ministry, *Order My Steps.* The Order My Steps Conference hosted its first international tour in Germany and Atlanta, USA, in 2004 and has held additional conferences in Jamaica and in the USA: Charlotte, North Carolina; Orlando, Florida; and Philadelphia, Pennsylvania.

Bishop Francis is the author of several outstanding books including: *Is There a Word from the Lord?, What Do You Do When You're Left Alone?, 10 Steps to Get out of Debt, The Pastors & Church Workers Handbook,* and has released four CDs entitled *Finally, Bishop John Francis, One Lord, One Faith, Manifestation of the Promise,* and the most current, *Welcome in this Place.*

Bishop Francis's wife, Penny, is the co-pastor of Ruach City Church and has worked alongside him throughout his ministry. They have three lovely daughters, Juanita, Teleisa, and Charisa.

MINISTRY CONTACT INFORMATION

Website
www.johnfrancis.org.uk

Phone
Ruach City Church
+44 (020) 8678 6888

Email: global@ruachcitychurch.org

Facebook: BishopJohnFrancis

Twitter: BishopJFrancis

Instagram: BishopJFrancis

OTHER BOOKS/CDS BY BISHOP JOHN FRANCIS

Is There a Word from the Lord?

What Do You Do When You're Left Alone?

10 Steps to Get out of Debt

The Pastors & Church Workers Handbook

FOUR MUSICAL CDS ENTITLED

Finally, Bishop John Francis

One Lord, One Faith

Manifestation of the Promise

Welcome in this Place

Contact Information

For additional copies of this book and other products from Cross House Books, contact: sales@crosshousebooks.co.uk.

Please visit our Website for product updates and news at www.crosshousebooks.co.uk.

OTHER INQUIRIES

CROSS HOUSE BOOKS

Christian Book Publishers
245 Midstocket Road, Aberdeen, AB15 5PH, UK

info@crosshousebooks.co.uk
publisher@crosshousebooks.co.uk

"The entrance of Your Word brings light."

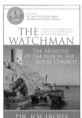

Times of Refreshing Volume 2

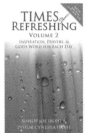

Times of Refreshing Volume 2 gives readers the ability to tap in to daily supernatural experiences! As with *Times of Refreshing Volume 1*, Volume 2 overflows with inspiring messages, comforting prayers, and Scriptures that bring His presence home. These daily boosts of God's love are just what the Divine Doctor ordered for a healthy mind, body, and spirit. Each page includes a Scripture and God-given message, as well as space for interactive exchanges of the reader's written word with His. An added bonus is a listing of Scriptures to read the Bible in a year. Prophetic Prayer Points conclude this volume of encouraging and motivating messages of daily living the supernatural, victorious life in God's Kingdom.

Times of Refreshing Volume 3

Each volume of *Times of Refreshing* is filled with daily inspiration, love, and hope. Beginning with a Scripture passage and followed with insights straight from the throne of God, readers worldwide have been strengthened and motivated to pursue their daily destiny. A few inspirational questions conclude the day's devotion, prompting a search into the inner being to discover truths from the Lord—nuggets of His devotion and wisdom. And for those who have never read the entire Bible, on every page are Scripture references from the Old and New Testaments so the Bible can be read in a year's time. Pastors Joe and Cynthia Ibojie authored *Times of Refreshing* out of united prayer and compassionate hearts.

Times of Refreshing Volume 4

Best-selling author Bishop Joe Ibojie and his wife, Pastor Cynthia Ibojie, have again combined their unique prophetic gifting with rare vision into the mysteries of God as they offer *Times of Refreshing Volume 4* for everyone yearning to find daily peace and solace by stepping into God's presence. As with the first three very popular volumes of *Times of Refreshing, Volume 4* includes a Scripture, Holy Spirit-inspired message, and questions designed to provoke thought and soothing meditation. There is also a convenient list of Scriptures so you can read the Bible in a year—everything you need to make each and every day a supernatural, victorious experience!

Revelations Training Manual

Revelations Training Manual takes you into the depths of God's holiness and desire to communicate with His children. It is possible to understand your dreams and revelations from God—and with the wisdom shared in this manual, your spiritual questions will be answered.

How You Can Live an Everyday Supernatural Life

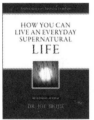

This comprehensive manual is the perfect training ground for every believer! Filled with practical and easy-to-implement ways to achieve a supernatural lifestyle, readers can immediately put into practice the God-given advice, insights, and revelations. Essential keys are presented that open the doors into a realm of divine and intimate relationship with God. He welcomes all to enjoy daily spiritual and physical miracles, signs, and wonders—naturally in the supernatural. Senior Pastor Joe Ibojie is a worldwide Bible and prophetic teacher.

Destined for the Top

Destined for the Top presents simple and proven successful answers to life's most complex questions. Divided into two parts—Life Issues and Family Issues—you can be at the top of your game in every aspect of your life by knowing what and who to avoid during your journey to the top. Through an added feature of thought-provoking questions at the end of each chapter, you will learn how to strengthen your spirit, invest in your potential, and realize how fickle your feelings really are. You will discover how God's wisdom and love through you propels you toward fulfilling your destiny!

The Final Frontiers—Countdown to the Final Showdown

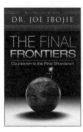

The Final Frontiers—Countdown to the Final Showdown peers profoundly into the future. It expertly explores the emerging cosmic involvement of the seemingly docile elements of nature and their potential to completely alter the ways of warfare. Christians must not allow the things that are supposed to bless them to become instruments of judgment or punishment. *The Final Frontiers* provides you with a practical approach to the changing struggles that confront humanity now and in your future.

The Watchman: The Ministry of the Seer in the Local Church

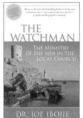

The ministry of the watchman in a local church is possibly one of the most common and yet one of the most misunderstood ministries in the Body of Christ. Over time, the majority of these gifted people have been driven into reclusive lives because of relational issues and confusion surrounding their very vital ministry in the local church.

The Justice of God: Victory in Everyday Living

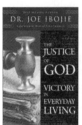

Only once in awhile does a book bring rare insight and godly illumination to a globally crucial subject. This book is one of them! A seminal work from a true practitioner, best-selling author, and leader of a vibrant church, Dr. Joe Ibojie brings clarity and a hands-on perspective to the Justice of God. *The Justice of God* reveals: How to pull down your blessings; How to work with angels; The power and dangers of prophetic acts and drama.

Illustrated Bible-Based Dictionary of Dream Symbols— BEST SELLER

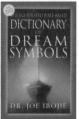

Illustrated Bible-Based Dictionary of Dream Symbols is much more than a book of dream symbols. This book is a treasure chest, loaded down with revelation and the hidden mysteries of God that have been waiting since before the foundation of the earth to be uncovered. Whether you use this book to assist in interpreting your dreams or as an additional resource for your study of the Word of God, you will find it a welcome companion.

EXPANDED AND ENRICHED WITH EXCITING NEW CONTENT

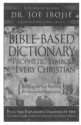

Bible-Based Dictionary of Prophetic Symbols for Every Christian—NEW

The most comprehensive, illustrated Bible-based dictionary of prophetic and dream symbols ever compiled is contained in this one authoritative book! *The Bible-Based Dictionary of Prophetic Symbols for Every Christian* is a masterpiece that intelligently and understandably bridges the gap between prophetic revelation and application—PLUS it includes the expanded version of the best selling *Illustrated Bible-Based Dictionary of Dream Symbols.*

How to Live the Supernatural Life in the Here and Now— BEST SELLER

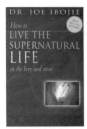

Are you ready to stop living an ordinary life? You were meant to live a supernatural life! God intends us to experience His power every day! In *How to Live the Supernatural Life in the Here and Now* you will learn how to bring the supernatural power of God into everyday living. Finding the proper balance for your life allows you to step into the supernatural and to move in power and authority over everything around you. Dr. Joe Ibojie, an experienced pastor and prolific writer, provides practical steps and instruction that will help you live a life of spiritual harmony.

Dreams and Visions Volume 1—BEST SELLER

Dreams and Visions presents sound scriptural principles and practical instructions to help you understand dreams and visions. The book provides readers with the necessary understanding to approach dreams and visions by the Holy Spirit through biblical illustrations, understanding of the meaning of dreams and prophetic symbolism, and by exploring the art of dream interpretation according to ancient methods of the Bible.

Available in Italian and Koream translations.

Dreams and Visions Volume 2

God speaks to you through dreams and visions. Do you want to know the meaning of your dreams? Do you want to know what He is telling and showing you? Now you can know! *Dreams and Visions Volume 2* is packed full of exciting and Bible-guided ways to discover the meaning of your God-inspired, dreamy nighttime adventures and your wide-awake supernatural experiences!

The Enemy Called Worry

Worry gives birth to many sins and affects a person's spiritual development and physical health. There is a way to eliminate worry from your life and move forward into your God-given destiny. This book gives you every weapon needed to proclaim victory over *The Enemy Called Worry!*

40 Names of the Holy Spirit

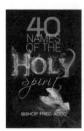

The names of God represent a deliberate *invitation to you* to take advantage of what God can and wants to be in your life. Whatever you call Him is what He will become to you. Do you know all of His names? How much deeper would you like to know the Comforter? You will learn: Seven Symbols of the Holy Spirit; Names of the Holy Spirit; Seven Things *Not* to Do to the Holy Spirit; Twentyfold Relationship with the Holy Spirit; Fourfold Presence of the Holy Spirit; Seven Keys to Receiving the Holy Spirit Baptism—and much more!

Growing God's Kingdom

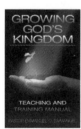

Written by an experienced Bible scholar and beloved pastor, the insights and depth of God's word is thoughtfully shared so that newborn Christians and mature believers alike can understand and appreciate. Prefaced with an intriguing prophecy, *Growing God's Kingdom* contains practical principles that reveal the importance of God's mandate to share the gospel. You will learn about being mentored and mentoring those next in line to inherit God's riches.